THE GARIMUS FILE

THE GARIMUS FILE

Written by
Gary Stanley

Illustrations by
John Hawk

Published by
HERE'S LIFE PUBLISHERS, INC.
San Bernardino, California 92402

THE GARIMUS FILE
A Back-Door Look at New Testament Times
by Gary Stanley

Published by
HERE'S LIFE PUBLISHERS, INC.
P.O. Box 1576
San Bernardino, CA 92402

Library of Congress Catalogue Card 82-072301
HLP Product No. 40-311-3

Printed in the United States of America

Much more than thanks
to Janet,
my teacher, editor
and friend.

CONTENTS

~~FOURWORD~~
~~FORWARD~~
FOREWORD

This book is the result of my vocal complaint that many written Bible studies are predictable. The Bible is far too fascinating and intriguing ever to be predictable. I made that statement once too often and was given the opportunity to put my pen where my mouth was. Here is my answer to that challenge.

The New Testament letters are like half a conversation. John, Paul and the rest assume their readers are familiar with current events, previous conversations or other writings that prompted their letters. Of course, we don't have the advantage of reading their letters with a first-century mind.

But due to a rare stroke of luck, we now have a new source of extrabiblical writings! Previously unpublished letters as well as other written documents have surfaced to shed some light on the circumstances surrounding the inspired writ. While the authenticity of these artifacts may be a bit shady, the resulting Bible study is anything but predictable....

1
The Little Brother

How would you like to be the little brother of someone who seemed practically perfect? You would get to follow him through school; he probably made all **A**'s. Whenever you get into an argument with him, you're always wrong. No matter what you do, no matter how hard you try, you always fall short of your brother's mark. Oh, you may be able to run faster or drive a nail straighter, but in the main qualities of life (character, credibility and confidence), you will never better your elder brother. You see, he never swears when he bangs his thumb with a hammer!

To make matters worse, he becomes a popular speaker and begins to imply that he is God incarnate. How embarrassing! Imagine trying to explain your brother to your friends. Finally, your family is disgraced when he is executed like a common criminal.

James had the dubious honor of being the little brother of Jesus.[1] Of course, James also had the privilege of living in the same household as Jesus. They went to the same school, they ate at the same table, and Mary watched over them both. Who more than James could view Christ under close scrutiny?

Such is the background of the author of the letter to the "twelve tribes who are dispersed abroad,"[2] the Epistle of James. It has been called everything from a "right strawy epistle"[3] to the Proverbs of the New Testament.

The following interview with James is an undated (and unconfirmed) document found recently in a file drawer:

1

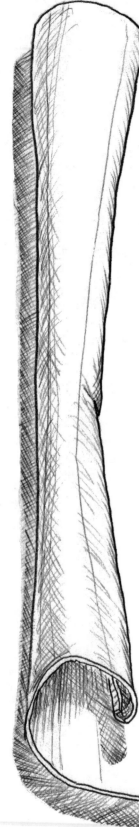

Garimus: Growing up around Jesus, did you ever think that there was something special about Him?

James: Every boy thinks his big brother is special, but not in the way you mean. He was always different I suppose, but remember, I grew up with Him, and life with Jesus was normal for me. But while familiarity can enhance many things, worship isn't usually one of them.

Garimus: What did your family think when Jesus began to receive so much publicity?

James: I'm not sure any of us gave it much thought at first. Jesus reacted pretty strongly to John the Baptist's preaching,[4] but many were moved by John's words. There were what we thought to be wild rumors about some wine at a wedding feast in Cana.[5] But the Sabbath when Jesus stood in the synagogue in Nazareth and read from the scroll—that was something else. He claimed that the portion of Scripture He had just read about the messiah was fulfilled in their hearing. It started a riot! Our friends and neighbors were so incensed at His blasphemy that they tried to throw Jesus off a cliff.[6] After that we were glad He moved to Capernaum.[7] We tried to tone Him down a couple of times, but He wouldn't listen.[8]

Garimus: Did you try to keep track of Him?

James: I didn't have to. Everyone was constantly telling us what Jesus had said or done.[9] I couldn't escape news of Him.

Garimus: Did you ever go to see Him for yourself?

James: Once. Jesus was speaking to a large crowd from the crest of a hill.[10] Everyone was so quiet you could hear every word a long way off. I sat under a tree at the edge of the crowd and just listened. I can still hear His exact words to this day.[11] Oh, did He make

me uncomfortable! My pride wouldn't let me accept what He said, but my heart wouldn't let me forget. So I avoided all possible contact with Him.[12]

Garimus: When did you change your mind?

James: I never did. Jesus changed my mind after He changed my heart. The trial and crucifixion were a nightmare.[13] Mother insisted on being there.[14] My brothers[15] and I all refused to take her, but she went anyway. Then, as if His death weren't enough, rumors began that Jesus had risen from the dead.[16] And that's when it happened...

Garimus: What happened?

James: Jesus appeared to me. My big brother presented me with conclusive proof of His claims—Himself.[17]

Garimus: It seems odd that you didn't mention being His brother in your letter. Why didn't you make more out of that fact?

James: I certainly didn't glory in being His brother during His earthly life. It hardly seems appropriate to claim such a title now. A "bondservant of God"[18] is what I am, and that is more honor than I can possibly bear.

Garimus: Still, you became the head of the church at Jerusalem.[19]

James: True, but my position wasn't based on nepotism. All of us enter into His service the same way, by faith alone.

Garimus: That brings up an interesting question. You are perhaps best known for your statement "Faith without works is dead."[20] How do you square that with your comment about "faith alone"?

James: I was wondering when we'd get around to that question. It's amusing that my little letter, almost totally devoid of theology, has become such a watershed for theological speculation. Thank God we are saved by proper faith and not by our theology!

Do you think it odd that Paul's affirmation of faith[21] and my insistence on works could be fast friends? Don't forget it was Paul who came to me for advice, not once but three times.[22] Paul, Barnabas and I, with several others, resolved much of this issue at the Council of Jerusalem.[23]

Garimus: And what was the consensus of that council?

James: That Jewish works and ritual aren't essential for salvation.[24] But I think one of my more favorable critics[25] summed up proper faith quite nicely when he said, "Faith alone saves, but saving faith is never alone."

Garimus: Was the council's decision what prompted you to write your epistle?

James: No. I actually wrote that letter several years before the meeting. A great persecution had broken out against the church in Jerusalem. Stephen was stoned, Saul was imprisoning those he could find, and the rest were being scattered abroad.[26] Some practical help was called for. No one had to be convinced of the theological implications of tribulation. They wanted to know how to deal with it and a host of other problems they would have to face without the support of their home church.

Garimus: Is there an underlying theme to your advice for all of those problems?

James: There certainly is! It is that the best advice in the world is worth nothing if it isn't acted on.[27] I could recite Jesus' Sermon on the Mount from memory, but it wasn't until I began to act on what He said years later that it made any real difference.[28]

Garimus: What's the most obvious difference your active faith has produced?

James: Well, they don't call me Old Camel Knees[29] for nothing.

Garimus: Old Camel Knees!

James: It refers to a lifetime of kneeling in prayer. Pastoring a church will drive anyone to his knees in prayer. Prayer is perhaps the only thing that truly combines faith and works. I'm not sure it can be done in any other way. I've never seen a successful petitioner who wasn't ready to take an active part in the answer to each of his prayers.[30]

Garimus: One last question. Tradition claims that you were martyred in Jerusalem by stoning at the hands of Ananius, the high priest.[31] Would you care to comment on that bit of tradition?

James: No, I don't see any reason to change that tradition at this time.

5

NOTE TO THE READER:

There's an old saying, "You can fool all of the people some of the time, and some of the people all of the time, but you can't fool Mom (or your brother)." That James was able to accept his half-brother as the Son of God is a powerful testimony. James' view of the Christian life is unique and demanding. Like James, most of us know far more than we are willing to act on.

As you work on correcting this malady, what nickname (such as James' nickname, "Old Camel Knees") would you like to represent your life of faith? Oh yes, you might want to write out some specific steps you plan to take to ensure the right name sticks.[32]

Garimus' Guide for Getting in Step with the Footnotes

Beneath the surface of these fictitious artifacts is a wealth of Bible study material. The footnotes are offered to help you dig out the material. Sometimes the footnotes refer to sources that merely break the ground for a bit of fanciful excavation. Others point to Bible verses that might be the New Testament writer's response to my dubious documentations. Either way, you will have to work the footnotes to get the justifications for my speculations. After reading one of my chapters, I recommend you read the New Testament letter being studied (in one sitting if possible). Then look up the footnotes. If a footnote directs you to a passage in the Bible, read the surrounding verses as well. There's nothing like knowing the context for them to make sense. It may even help you answer the questions at the end of the study.

FOOTNOTES

1. Mark 6:3. Actually, James was the half-brother of Jesus (James' father was Joseph), and there were three other brothers and at least two sisters.
2. James 1:1.
3. Martin Luther is said to have called James "a right strawy epistle."
4. Matthew 3:13—4:11; Luke 4:1-15.
5. John 2:1-11.
6. Luke 4:16-30.
7. Luke 4:31; Matthew 4:13.
8. John 7:3-6; Matthew 12:46-50.
9. Luke 4:14-15.
10. Matthew 5:1—7:27.
11. James alludes to the Sermon on the Mount more than 20 times in his brief epistle.
12. John 7:5.
13. The arrest, trial and crucifixion are found in Matthew 26:57—27:61; Mark 14:46—15:47; Luke 22:54—23:56; John 18:12—19:42.
14. John 19:26.

15. Judas, Joses and Simon (Mark 6:3).
16. The resurrection is recorded in Matthew 28:1-20; Mark 16:1-20; Luke 24:1-53; John 20:1—21:25; 1 Corinthians 15:4-6.
17. 1 Corinthians 15:7.
18. James 1:1.
19. James' leadership is clear from Acts 12:17; 15:13-21; and 21:18.
20. James 2:17, 26.
21. Romans 3:28; 5:1; Ephesians 2:8.
22. Acts 15:2; 21:18; Galatians 1:19.
23. Acts 15:1-19.
24. Acts 15:1-19; Galatians 2:9.
25. John Calvin.
26. Acts 8:1-3.
27. James 1:22.
28. Acts 1:14 indicates that Jesus' entire family believed on Him after His resurrection, and Acts 2:1 implies they were there on the day of Pentecost.
29. Eusebius, *Ecclesiastical History,* 2:23.
30. James 2:15-16.
31. Josephus, *Antiquities,* 20:9.1.
32. It has taken years for a friend of mine to live down his nickname, "The Bald Eagle of ISOT." Anatomically speaking, he never will.

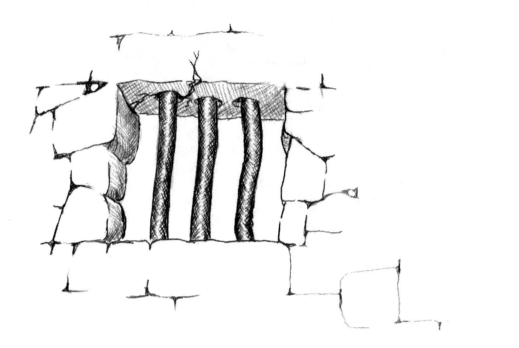

8

2
The Burden of Great Potential

It has been said that the surest road to failure is trying to please all the people all the time. That was not one of Paul's problems. A more checkered career, by the world's standards, would be hard to imagine. Revivals and riots followed him throughout his life.

That propensity to polarized potential was Paul's propositional polemic.* As one of the Peanuts gang put it, "There is nothing quite so burdensome as great potential." Potential never resides on only one side of the coin. Perhaps the most telling case is that of the archangel Lucifer. He had all the gifts necessary to be an angel of light, but discovered his abilities could also be used to rule the realms of darkness. Potential can easily cut either way.

After perusing Paul's personnel file (postulated, of course) the following two documents were uncovered. They are offered as partial proof of the double edge of potential.

10

---

*My humblest apologies for the verbosity, but I so wanted to get at least one of these past the editors.

OUTSTANDING YOUNG MEN OF JUDAH

March, A.D. 32

We are happy to announce that you have been recognized as an Outstanding Young Man of Judah by one of our board members, RABBI GAMALIEL. Please complete the following form for our publication.

Name: _Tentus[1]_ _Saul[2]_ _Ben[ ]_
           last name   first   middle

Home Town: _Tarsus[3]_ Province: _Cilicia[4]_ Citizenship: _Roman[5]_

Birth Date: _11 - 2_ , _A.D.2[6]_
          month day   year

Occupation: _teacher[7] tentmaker[8]_

Spouse: _Hester (deceased)[9]_

Children: _None_ , _____ , _____

Parents: _Gabe and Beth Tentus_ _(Osehohel)[10]_
                                     (family name if different)

Siblings: _Anna[11]_ , _____ , _____

Education

Name of School or University (List most recent first)	Degree or Diploma	Year Begun	Year Ended
Gamaliel's Rabbinical School of the Torah[12]	Doctor of Law	A.D.15	A.D.29
First Synagogue School of Tarsus[13]	Diploma	A.D.8	A.D.15[14]

Memberships (Clubs: school, civic, religious)

Name of Organization	Office Held	Year Begun	Year Ended
Pharisees[15]	Member (Active)[16]	A.D.28	Present
School Debate Team[17]	President	A.D.26	A.D.29
Greek Philosophy Club[18]	Secretary	A.D.25	A.D.27
Hillel Herald[19] (school paper)	Reporter	A.D.21	A.D.23

Honors and Awards

Organization Presenting Award	Award/Honor	Year Received
Gamaliel's Rabbinical School	Graduated Magna cum Laude [20]	A.D. 29
Aegean Games Commission	Bronze Medal (boxing) [21]	A.D. 20
First Synagogue School of Tarsus	Voted Most Likely to Succeed	A.D. 15

Publications (books, journal/magazine articles, etc.)

Title	Publisher	Year
Dangers in Damascus [22]	Damascus Theological Journal	A.D. 32
Saul's Political Satire (a weekly column)	Hillel Herald	A.D. 21-23

Hobbies and Interests

Travel. [23] Reading. History. Greek Philosophy.

Sailing. [24] Field and Track. [25] Writing [26]

12

Your name in your own hand is necessary to validate this document.

Signature: _Saul Ben Tentus_
(I certify to the truthfulness of this information)

Please return to:
OUTSTANDING YOUNG MEN OF JUDAH
Temple Place P.O. Box 144
Jerusalem, Judah

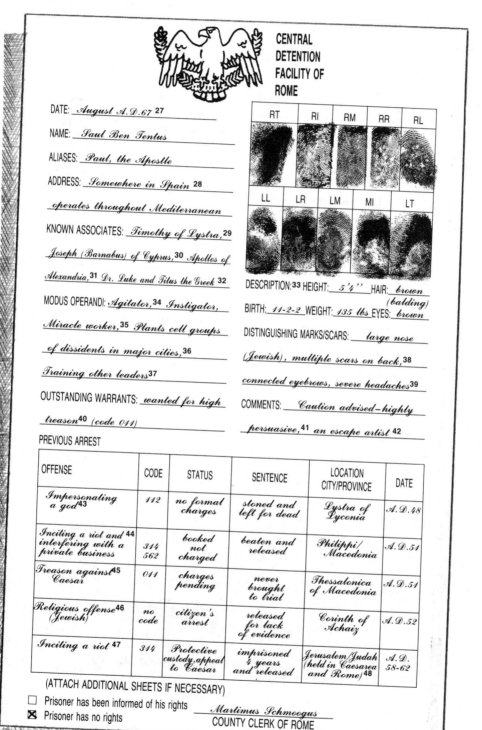

CENTRAL DETENTION FACILITY OF ROME

DATE: _August A.D. 67_ [27]

NAME: _Saul Ben Tentus_

ALIASES: _Paul, the Apostle_

ADDRESS: _Somewhere in Spain_ [28]

operates throughout Mediterranean

KNOWN ASSOCIATES: _Timothy of Lystra,_ [29]

Joseph (Barnabus) of Cyprus, [30] _Apollos of_

Alexandria, [31] _Dr. Luke and Titus the Greek_ [32]

MODUS OPERANDI: _Agitator,_ [34] _Instigator,_

Miracle worker, [35] _Plants cell groups_

of dissidents in major cities, [36]

Training other leaders[37]

OUTSTANDING WARRANTS: _wanted for high_

treason[40] _(code 011)_

RT	RI	RM	RR	RL
LL	LR	LM	MI	LT

DESCRIPTION:[33] HEIGHT: _5'4''_ HAIR: _brown_
(balding)

BIRTH: _11-2-2_ WEIGHT: _135 lbs_ EYES: _brown_

DISTINGUISHING MARKS/SCARS: _large nose_

(Jewish), multiple scars on back, [38]

connected eyebrows, severe headaches[39]

COMMENTS: _Caution advised – highly_

persuasive, [41] _an escape artist_ [42]

13

PREVIOUS ARREST

OFFENSE	CODE	STATUS	SENTENCE	LOCATION CITY/PROVINCE	DATE
Impersonating a god[43]	112	_no formal charges_	_stoned and left for dead_	_Lystra of Lyconia_	_A.D. 48_
Inciting a riot and interfering with a private business [44]	314 562	_booked not charged_	_beaten and released_	_Philippi/ Macedonia_	_A.D. 51_
Treason against Caesar [45]	011	_charges pending_	_never brought to trial_	_Thessalonica of Macedonia_	_A.D. 51_
Religious offense[46] _(Jewish)_	_no code_	_citizen's arrest_	_released for lack of evidence_	_Corinth of Achaiz_	_A.D. 52_
Inciting a riot [47]	314	_Protective custody, appeal to Caesar_	_imprisoned 4 years and released_	_Jerusalem/Judah (held in Caesarea and Rome)_ [48]	_A.D. 58-62_

(ATTACH ADDITIONAL SHEETS IF NECESSARY)

☐ Prisoner has been informed of his rights
☒ Prisoner has no rights

Martimus Schmoogus
COUNTY CLERK OF ROME

NOTE TO THE READER:

The burden of great potential is often the specter of what might have been. Paul was seldom burdened by that specter. The reality of his strategy to reach the world was almost equalled by his enemies' plans to stop him. The Christian life is not meant to be a passive existence but a bold endeavor. And the measure of success is set against a far greater standard than that of the world's. Perhaps Theodore Roosevelt was looking beyond the world's standards when he said:

"Far better it is to dare mighty things, win glorious triumphs even though checkered with failure than to rank with those poor spirits who neither enjoy much nor suffer much because they live in the gray twilight that knows neither victory nor defeat."

14 See **Garimus' Guide for Getting in Step with the Footnotes,**

which appears on page 6.

FOOTNOTES

1. A poor attempt at Latinizing the family trade.
2. Acts 13:9.
3. Acts 21:39.
4. *Ibid.*
5. Acts 22:27-28.
6. Acts 7:58 says that Paul was a young man. That could mean any age under 30. At 30, a Jewish man was considered mature and capable of leadership. Paul's leadership in the persecution of Christians in Damascus around A.D. 32 at least hints that he was close to that age.
7. 2 Timothy 1:11, in light of Paul's training under Gamaliel (Acts 22:3), suggests that he was trained as a teacher.
8. Acts 18:3.
9. There is no clear evidence either way. Some argue from silence i.e., it doesn't say he wasn't married. Of course, it doesn't say he was.
10. *Osehohel* is Hebrew for "tentmaker," a plausible family name. Perhaps

Paul's grandfather performed some valuable tentmaking service for the Roman cause, was granted citizenship and changed his name. For more information, see F. F. Bruce, *Paul: Apostle of the Heart Set Free*, Grand Rapids, Mich.: Wm. B. Eerdmans Publishing Co., 1978, p. 37.

11. Acts 23:16.
12. Acts 22:3.
13. *Ibid.*
14. Paul probably began his training in Jerusalem at the age of 13.
15. Acts 23:6; Philippians 3:5.
16. Acts 9:1-30.
17. This seemed to be one of Paul's favorite activities. Acts 17:22-32 suggests he was very good as a debater.
18. Galatians 1:16 and Ephesians 3:1 state Paul's calling to and interest in the Gentiles. Acts 17:2-4 shows his effectiveness among the Greeks.
19. Hillel was likely the father or grandfather of Gamaliel and the founder of one of the two leading schools of Pharisaism, the other being the Shammai school.
20. Galatians 1:14.
21. 1 Corinthians 9:26.
22. Acts 9:1-2.
23. Paul made at least three extensive missionary journeys, described in Acts 13-20.
24. Acts 27:21-22.
25. 1 Corinthians 9:24-27; 2 Timothy 4:7.
26. Paul wrote at least 13 New Testament books.
27. Paul probably died during this year.
28. Paul wanted to go to Spain, but his imprisonment in Caesarea and Rome forced him to postpone his trip. If Paul, in fact, was released from Rome, he may have gone to Spain before his final imprisonment and death in Rome.
29. Acts 16:1-3.
30. Acts 13:1-3.
31. 1 Corinthians 16:12.
32. Luke is mentioned by name only three times in Scripture (Colossians 4:14; Philemon 24; and 2 Timothy 4:11). Titus is mentioned in many of Paul's epistles. Some scholars speculate that these two were brothers.
33. Paul wasn't a particularly impressive figure to behold (2 Corinthians 10:10), and a second-century writer describes him as "a man of small stature, with a bald head and crooked legs, in a good state of body, with eyebrows meeting and nose somewhat hooked, full of grace" (The apocryphal *Acts of Paul and Thecla*).
34. Acts 21:40; 22:22.
35. Acts 14:10; 20:9-10; 28:3-5.
36. Acts 15:36.
37. 2 Timothy 2:2.

38. 2 Corinthians 11:24.
39. 2 Corinthians 12:7 speaks of Paul's thorn in the flesh. Speculations on the nature of the "thorn" are quite varied, ranging from the assertion that it was his wife to the suggestion that he had had a case of malaria. A popular theory is that Paul suffered from headaches that impaired his vision.
40. Presumably the charge for which Paul was ultimately executed.
41. Acts 26:28.
42. Acts 9:24-25; 17:2-14.
43. Acts 14:8-20.
44. Acts 16:11-40.
45. Acts 17:1-9.
46. Acts 18:12-17.
47. Acts 21:27—22:30.
48. Acts 23:33; 24:27; 28:16, 30.

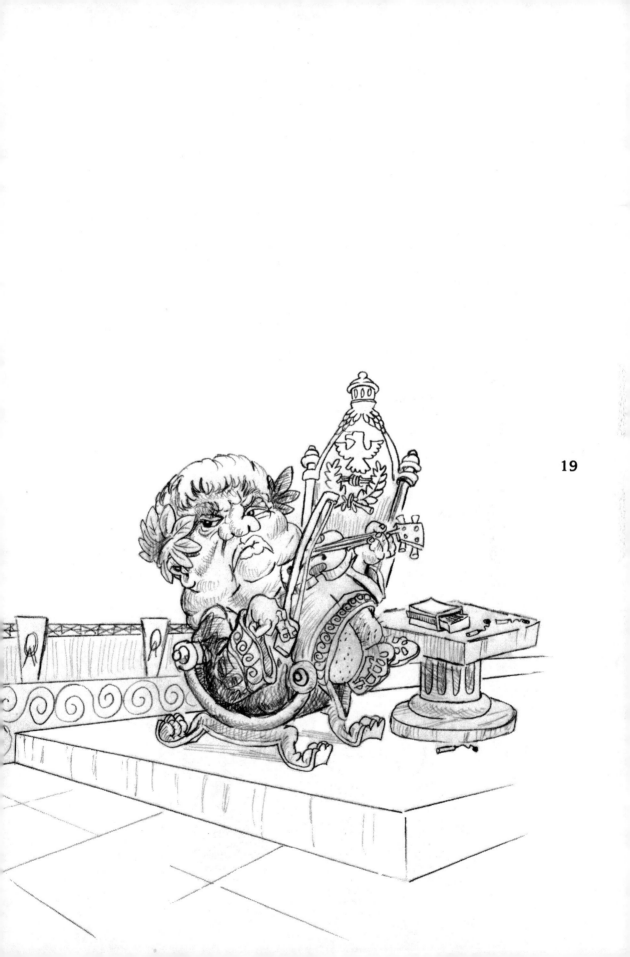

3
The Test Case

More than one-fourth of the entire New Testament (Luke and Acts) was written to a man named Theophilus, and that is all we know about him. Many theories about his identity have been offered. Some consider Theophilus to be nothing more than a literary device used to address all friends of God, because the name means "friend of God." Others suggest that Theophilus was the secret Christian name for Titus Flavius Clemens, a cousin to the Emperor Domitian.[1] But it is just possible that Theophilus was a Roman official involved in the judicial system—a defense lawyer who penned the following letter:

COL. A.A. THEOPHILUS (RET.)
Attorney at Law

Dear Dr. Luke,[2]

I must admit to being less than thrilled with the news of my appointment as Paul of Tarsus' defense council. My backlog of cases from the last administration is years from completion,[3] and the thought of defending a religious leader left me nauseated. But, having now read your detailed brief on the life of your messiah,[4] I must tell you how intrigued and honored I am to represent your friend. You have written a most persuasive document.

With Paul's colorful personality and the potentially explosive nature of the trial, any positive opinion persuaders like your "Gospel" will prove invaluable. The publicity afforded the case may well prove both a blessing and a bane.[5] The publicity will certainly help guarantee Paul a fair trial, but it may also work to negate the possibility of clemency should Paul be found guilty. Historically the caesars have viewed public displays of mercy in the courtroom as a sign of weakness.

In light of the indiscretions taken with Roman law in regard to Paul's arrest and imprisonment,[6] I have petitioned the court to drop all charges. It is unlikely in a case of this nature that my motion for dismissal will stand, but it is certainly worth a try. If the case comes to trial, let us hope and pray that an early date is set. I can foresee a time when hard evidence will carry little weight against the whims of the Emperor.[7] This Christianity of yours (and now mine) may soon become the scapegoat for all the ills of the Empire.[8]

I have carefully studied the notes made by Festus concerning the investigation.[9] But, aside from Claudius Lysias' written account of Paul's arrest,[10] there is precious little in the way of documented evidence from which to build a defense.

There are many avenues we might use to plead our case. But I need more background information about my new faith in order to prepare the best defense. Where did the church begin? Have any other leaders been arrested, and if so, what was the outcome?[11] And eyewitnesses— Luke, there are bound to be those willing to testify or at least make an official statement.[12]

Surely other Roman officials have responded as I; we are not the dull race you Greeks like to think we are. It seems clear from the record that the proconsul Gallio[13] and even Porcius Festus[14] have some respect for evidence presented by Paul in his own defense. However, with the change of venue,[15] everyone is now two thousand miles from the scene of the "crime."[16] I'm afraid that much of our court battle will be against the illusive opponents of guilt by association and public opinion. Luke, you know Paul far better than I, and much rests on our ability to portray him as a man of high moral character and honesty. Nero[17] will look at the episodes surrounding Paul's preaching and judge him as either the victim of Jewish zealots[18] or as the instigator of numerous riots. Quite frankly, on the surface it looks as though Paul used the local jails as his own private motel chain.

Officially, there is really only one charge to which Paul must answer, and it's minor in the eyes of a Roman court.[19] Despite the eloquent presentation by the attorney Tertullus,[20] what can they possibly make of a desecration charge to a Jewish temple? After all, this is a Gentile court with little sympathy for the Jews! Unofficially though, the real issue of the trial is the purported threat of Christianity in general (and Paul in particular) to the Roman Empire.[21]

Since Paul has insisted on making this trial a test case for all of Christianity,[22] we have much more to explain than a single incident. As you pointed out in your previous correspondence, this threat to Rome was precisely the charge that effectively placed Jesus on a Roman cross.[23] Pilate's apparent fear of Jewish unrest obviously clouded his judgment, and the wrong verdict was handed down.[24] Not only was an innocent man executed, but the Roman courts were manipulated into the unwitting role of accomplice in this travesty, as well.

It is quite possible for a similar fate to overtake Paul. There is more than ample evidence to convict Paul of being a Christian. And I do not think that Paul is remotely willing to soften his statements even to save his own life. He will likely want to present his testimony in such a way that it either convicts the officials of the court or incenses them.[25] Revivals and riots seem to be the natural order of events surrounding Paul. Do you really think the trial will be any different from all those other times? From what you've told me, our apostle will show little concern for his own person in his defense of the gospel.[26] However, Paul has so intricately and consistently woven his life together with the gospel that I can't imagine defending one and not the other.

While all the evidence against Paul is circumstantial, a lawyer like Tertullus could build a fairly substantial *prima facie* case.[27] That could be enough to convict Paul if the Emperor feels that he is a subversive or that Christianity could threaten the empire. So, what must be countered is any attempt by Tertullus to portray Paul as a fanatic. Only you know how hard that will be, given Paul's single-minded life-style. That story about Paul's reentering a city in which he had just been stoned to finish his sermon is commendable,[28] but what I need are documented accounts of Paul as a model prisoner[29] and a hero at sea.[30]

Finally, there is this matter of Paul's constantly appealing to a "higher source" for direction.[31] If we are to bring up the indwelling Spirit of God (and if we don't, Paul certainly will), it had better be judiciously done. Nero could easily view the miraculous anointing of men like Peter and Paul as a threat to his own divine claims.[32] And yet, as I understand it, it is precisely the work of God's Spirit in Paul's life that supplies the true motive for all of his activities.[33] I know that I'm just a babe in the faith, but it seems to me that God's Spirit quickens a servant's heart and not a kingly attitude.[34] If only Nero could understand that, he would see that Paul is no threat to him.

Luke, I think we have a good chance of winning this case.[35] We will be walking a fine line between the questionable tactics of the prosecution and an obligation to absolute honesty by the defense. I'll grant that in the past I have often been more concerned with the letter of the law than the spirit, but it is refreshing to share a common conviction for the truth and nothing but the truth. I'm beginning to wonder if Paul doesn't think it's really Caesar who will be on trial. Paul was certainly right when he said that there is a higher court than Caesar's.[36]

23

Sincerely yours,

A. A. Theophilus

Theophilus, LL.D

P.S. Thank you for sending that marvelous ointment; these old bones aren't what they used to be.[37] Oh yes, be sure to dispose of this letter; it could be devastating if it fell into the wrong hands.

NOTE TO THE READER:

Many scholars think that Paul was released from prison (Theophilus won his case) and was able to travel on to Spain. During his five-year reprieve, he was able to write to both Timothy and Titus before his final imprisonment and death in A.D. 67.

Luke's response to this letter can be found in the New Testament book of Acts. How much evidence do you think the prosecuting attorney, Tertullus, could find to convict you of practicing your faith? And what would Luke include in your defense to show the Holy Spirit's directing your life? From personal experience, I suggest a plea of "no contest" while throwing yourself on the mercy of the court. After all, the greatest truth is that our trial is already over and the mercy of God is ours for the asking.

See **Garimus' Guide for Getting in Step with the Footnotes,**

which appears on page 6.

FOOTNOTES

1. See Huber L. Drumwright, *Saints Alive! The Humble Heros of the New Testament* (Nashville: Broadman, 1972), pp. 62-66.
2. Colossians 4:14.
3. Nero's lack of interest in administration likely congested the court list for the first six years of his rule. See A. N. Sherwin-White, *Roman Society & Roman Law in the New Testament* (Grand Rapids, MI: Baker Book House, 1978, repr. of 1963 ed.), p. 118.
4. Luke's gospel.
5. Philippians 1:12-13.
6. Acts 22:25,29.
7. Nero's rule was a mixture of merriment and murder. See John Foxe, *Foxe's Christian Martyrs of the World* (Chicago: Moody, n.d.), pp. 36-40.
8. Christians were accused of burning Rome, although Nero himself did it.
9. Acts 25:26.

10. Acts 23:26-30.
11. Acts 4:1-23; 5:17-25; 6:8-15; 12:1-11; 16:19-33.
12. Acts 5:33-42; 10:1-31; 18:8; 25:25; 26:32.
13. Acts 18:12-17.
14. Acts 25:25.
15. Acts 25:12.
16. Acts 21:28.
17. Acts 27:24. Nero was ruling (A.D. 54 to 68) during Paul's imprisonment.
18. Acts 9:23; 13:50; 17:5; 18:12; 20:3; 23:20; 25:3.
19. Acts 25:18-19.
20. Acts 24:2-8.
21. Acts 25:8.
22. Acts 26:6.
23. Luke 23:2.
24. Luke 23:22-24.
25. Acts 26:28.
26. Acts 20:24.
27. Evidence sufficient to raise a presumption of fact.
28. Acts 14:19-20.
29. Acts 16:27-28; 27:3; 28:30.
30. Acts 27:31-44.
31. Acts 26:19.
32. Nero claimed to be a god. See *Persecution in the Early Church*, Herbert Workman, Oxford Univ. Press, 1980, p 40.
33. Acts 22:10.
34. Luke 9:46-48.
35. Philippians 1:25-26.
36. 2 Timothy 4:1.
37. Theophilus' title "most excellent" (Luke 1:3), was used to designate a Roman cavalry officer, and saddle sores are a universal hazard.

4
The Handwriting on the Wall

Graffiti has been with us since man first learned to scribble. In fact, the word *graffito* means "to scribble or scratch." It was coined by archaeologists to describe the casual writings that have covered everything from the great monuments of ancient Egypt to the subways of New York.

In the ancient Roman world, only the more important documents and letters were written on the scarce and costly paper of the day (papyrus). The writings of everyday life found their way to the outer plaster walls of public and private buildings throughout the Empire.[1]

The subject matter of ancient graffiti was as varied as the lives of the people who put it there. Election notices, advertisements, love notes, grocery lists, lewd limericks and religious slogans all were there to greet the passer-by. Even God has written on a wall or two.[2]

As Paul made his way through the regions of Pamphylia, Pisidia and southern Galatia,[3] he was doubtless aware of the handwriting on the walls. The thoughts and sentiments of his audiences scribbled on the walls provided a valuable critique on the effectiveness of his message.

27

Who knows? Perhaps Paul read some of this graffiti on his way out of town, and it later prompted him to pen his first letter to the churches of Galatia. The following collection of graffiti was supposedly found on a building adjacent to a Jewish synagogue where Paul was reported to have spoken.

GOD IS DEAD

ZENUS IS DEAD

ZENUS IS DEAD GOD [4]

THE ONLY GOOD GENTILE IS A CIRCUMSIZED ONE [5]

So What? [7]

Abraham was a Gentile [6]

YEA, but he was circumsized

LONG LIVE THE LAW [9]

CLAVDIVS IS A FINK [8]

long live Life!

Life Stinks!

the Law stinks

Gentiles Stink!

Spartacus was right

Jews are just a cut above the rest.

"Admiror, paries, te non cecidisse ruinis, qui tot scriptorum Taedia Sosfineas [10]

DAVIS

GRACE ISN'T cheap [11]

But its free

NOTHING IS free [12]

Grace

LEAGLIZE PROSTITUTION [13]

K SM H

DON'T MISS THE LAST DAYS OF POMPEII

NOW SHOWING IN THE AMPHITHEATER

It's great! You should see it.

MIMUS

Titus Hostilius Welches on his bets

PLATVS

Tarquinius Superbus is a liar [14]

XII
XIII
IV
XXXVII
XXXXI
VII
TAX
XVI

IF YOU CAN READ THIS THE BLOOD IS RUSHING TO YOUR HEAD.

28

SLAVE SALE

EVERY THRUSDAY AT

MARKET STREET →

FREE ME! [15]

Free Beer ~~Beer~~ NOTHING IS FREE

HI

Freedom is a myth [16]

A Promise is a Promise

MARCUS

~~APION~~

+

Helen

PAUL IS A SICKEY [17]

There was a young man named Saul.
Who changed his First name to Paul
It didn't make him an Apostle
Or anything So Colossal
Just a fellow with an awful lot of gall. [19]

LEVI was Here

Jesus Saves [20]

WHAT? ↑ Coupons Dummy

JESUS IS ALIVE AND WELL [18]

and living in Cypress

ROMANS GO HOME [21]

The Golden Rule
He who has The Gold rules [22]

Cute →

For a real good time call VIII VIII VI — VII IX VIII I

BRVTVS

Paul go Home [23]

Suckers get hooked

the best fruit is The Fruit of The Vine [25]

Amen!

For a good time meet me at the Temple of Venus [24]

Cassondra →

She didn't show [26]

G.I. C.L.

29

NOTE TO THE READER:

Graffiti hasn't changed much in the last 2,000 years. Neither has man. He's still trying to work his way into God's favor.

After Paul's first missionary journey, a dispute over the question of freedom began to circulate among the churches of Galatia. Can the gospel that Paul preached operate independent of the Jewish Law? In other words, is anything really free?

It was the threat of a different gospel that compelled Paul to write his firs letter to a church.[27]

Apparently a group of Judaizers were saying that the gospel was valid only if one first became a Jew (i.e., was circumcised and lived under the Law). The modern-day version of this perversion is only slightly different from its ancient ancestor: it claims you must clean up your life before God will accept you, and you'd better keep it clean if you want to keep His love.

Paul clearly demonstrates throughout his letter that salvation is based solely on one's response to Christ. It still is. As the saying goes, "God's grace isn't cheap—but it is free." I recommend the following bit of graffiti for your consideration and memorization. You may be freer than you think.[28].

Do this and live
the Law demands,
But gives me neither
feet nor hands.
A better word
the gospel brings,
It bids me fly
and gives me wings.

Author Untraceable[29]

See **Garimus' Guide for Getting in Step with the Footnotes,**

which appears on page 6.

FOOTNOTES

1. An interesting account on graffiti is found in Amadeo Maiuri's *Pompeii,* page 18ff (published by Istituto Poligrafico Dello Stato in Rome, 1970, translated by W. F. MacCormick, 14th edition), a guidebook to the museums, galleries and monuments of Italy. The book and the idea for this chapter both belong to my roommate, Marty Schoenleber.
2. Daniel 5:5,24.
3. After a bit of island hopping, Paul traveled through the southern portions of Asia Minor on his first missionary journey (Acts 13-1—14:28).
4. Galatians 6:7.
5. The Judaizers were insisting that the Gentiles first become Jews (be circumcised) and *then* become Christians (Galatians 2:3; 5:6,11,12; 6:12,13,15).
6. Paul uses Abraham as a prime example of justification by faith and not works (Galatians 3:6,11).
7. Galatians 3:28.
8. Tiberius Claudius Germanicus was emperor of Rome from A.D. 41 to 54. His programs to restore the ancient religions of Rome resulted in the expulsion of Jews and Christians alike from the city of Rome (Acts 18:2).
9. Some were saying that salvation came through the Law. For Paul's response, see Galatians 2:16; 3:3,10-12; 5:3,4.
10. "It is a wonder, O Wall, that thou has not yet crumbled under the weight of so much written nonsense" (Maiuri, *Pompeii,* page 20.)
11. The price of God's grace is one Son (Galatians 2:20).
12. Galatians 3:23-25.
13. Paul gives a list of moral problems evident in Galatia (Galatians 5:19-21) and admonishes his readers to walk in the Spirit (Galatians 5:13, 16).
14. *Ibid.*
15. Galatians 5:1.
16. Paul develops the priority of God's grace in Jesus over the Jewish concept of the Law in Galatians 3:15-29. The Promise came before the Law (3:17), and the Law was given as a tutor for the intermediate period before the coming of the Promised One (3:19,24,25).
17. Galatians 4:13-14.
18. Galatians 1:1; 2:20
19. A Jewish group was trying to subvert Paul's authority (Galatians 5:10) as an apostle, and ultimately to subvert his message of faith in Jesus (1:6). Paul lists three distinct credentials to prove his claim to apostleship: his revelation from Jesus (1:11-24); his apostolic endorsement from Peter, James and John (2:1-10); and his personal integrity (2:11-21).
20. Galatians 3:1-15.
21. The author who coined this slogan has asked that his name be withheld for health reasons.
22. Galatians 5:14.
23. Galatians 4:16-18.

24. See footnote 13.
25. Galatians 5:22-23.
26. This mark is the first part of an identification code system used by early Christians. One person would draw it in the sand, and if the other person was a Christian, he would add the other line, completing the drawing of a fish.
27. This was such an important issue that within a year of the writing of Galatians the first Council of Jerusalem (Acts 15) was held to address this problem.
28. Galatians 3:1-5 says that even our spiritual growth is the result of faith and not works.
29. Recently confirmed during a phone call to J. Sidlow Baxter.

34

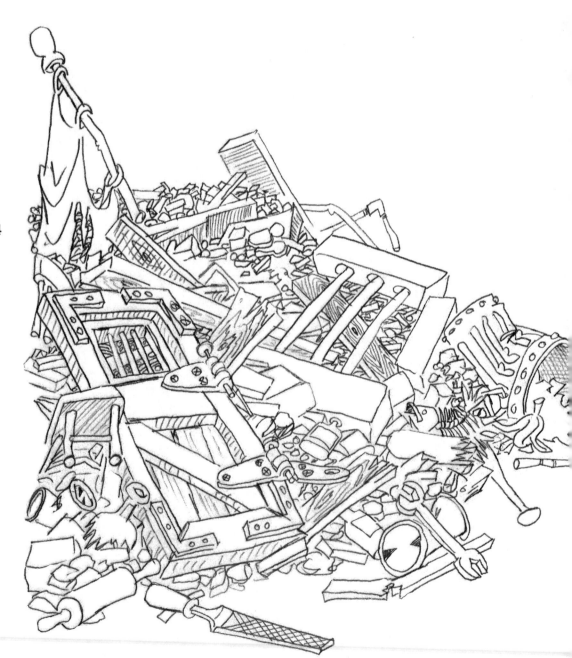

5
Riots and Revivals

Newspapers have their own type of morgue. The file of clippings from back issues can fill an entire room. The morgue is like a dead letter box—one never knows what may be unearthed from beneath several layers of dust.

The backdrop to a famous Pauline letter was recently resurrected from the decayed newspaper vaults in the ancient city of Thessalonica. Paul's letter seems a fitting response to the concerns reported in the clippings. Paul's epistle surfaces the timeless themes of hope and assurance. And, as the following clippings chronicle, events of despair and destruction were unfolding in the city. (The veracity and historicity of the following newspaper clippings is neither expressed nor implied by this editor.)

Religion Section

Thessalonica averages at least two circuses, crusades or campaigns every month. This month is no exception as the itinerant preacher, Paul of Tarsus, begins his crusade in our city.[2]

Paul's message contends that a common carpenter, executed by a Roman court more than 15 years ago, is the long-awaited savior of the Jews (and anyone else who is interested). To date Paul has restricted his proclamations to the local synagogues,[3] and his message is being well received among the Greek proselytes and not a few leading women.[4]

How these events will set with the local Jewish leaders is not hard to predict. The head rabbi stated his position: "During the time of this carpenter named Jesus there were no less than 40 men who claimed to be the messiah of the Jews.[5] It is no more likely that this particular contender is the messiah than that he could be raised from the dead.[6]

It is further reported that Paul claims this Jesus will soon be returning to collect his followers.[7] Perhaps Paul's crusade should be exhibited under the entertainment section of this paper.

37

THE THESSALONICAN TATTLER
"all the news that fits"

vol. LXVII   Thursday March 15 A.D.51

RIOTS IN THE STREETS

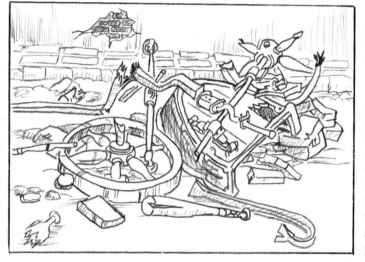

What do earthquakes,[8] riots,[9] and charges of high treason[10] have in common? If an abundance of rumors and a few police reports are to be believed, the answer is Paul of Tarsus, an itinerant preacher.

Last night a mob formed in the main marketplace above Harbor Street and made its way along the Egnatian Way to the house of a local merchant[11] where Paul was reported to be staying. By the time the authorities stepped in to stop the fighting, more than a dozen men were injured, three seriously. Five arrests were made. Two were inebriated Corinthian sailors, charged with disturbing the

peace and destroying public property; the other three were of Paul's group,[12] arrested on suspicion of high treason.

One of the sailors offered his version of the riot from his prison cell: "Me and my mates here was having a friendly brew at the Bacchus Bar and Grill, when we heard a commotion in the street. Some locals was hollering about spies and traitors and the like. Jake and me thought there might be a stoning or at least a scourging afoot."

The sailor further explained, "Of course it was our civic duty to go along and help defend the empire;[13] I'm a vet, you

know! They had no cause to arrest us," he concluded. "Besides, how was we to know that it was a guard's chariot we trashed? They all look alike in the dark!"

One of those being held on suspicion of treason is Jason, the owner of the house where the disturbance occurred. When queried about the validity of the charges and his association with Paul, he responded, "The thought of Paul's being a threat to Caesar or anyone else is absurd. As Paul so carefully pointed out, following Jesus is a spiritual and not a political matter.[14]

"Although Paul was here but a few weeks,[15]" Jason went on to say, "it's hard to imagine a more humble or caring man.[16] He was a giver, not a taker,[17] and one had only to look in his eyes to know."

Jason summed up, "How can anyone condemn the noble ideals of faith, hope and love Paul preaches?[18] The whole

Please see RIOTS, B-8

★*RIOTS*

continued from A-1

issue should be settled any day now, for when our God comes to take us home the truth will be known."[19]

Shortly after the arrest, Jason posted bail for himself and his two companions,[20] pledging to avoid any further confrontations or contact with the local synagogue.

One of those charging Paul and his followers with treason issued the following statement: "The Jewish community in no way endorses this fanatical movement and summarily condemns any of its actions.[21]

"This Paul is preying on the weaknesses of women and the gullibility of our Greek converts[22] to turn them away from the faith of our fathers," the spokesman continued. "I un-derstand that he was recently thrown in jail after a similar riot in Philippi.[23] He is a danger to our whole society."

The spokesman said, "He has claimed allegiance to another king, Jesus, a criminal himself who was tried and executed by a Roman court."

Paul of Tarsus was not among those arrested and was unavailable for comment.[24] The authorities have issued a warrant for his arrest along with his two traveling companions, Silas and Timothy.[25]

Monday April 30 A.D. 51
page 8
Economic Section

While all the major economic indicators show an increase of productivity in our area, a significant number of workers are now without jobs.

A local union representative states, "Jobs are in plentiful supply even with the unfair competition of slave labor. However, several members of our union have walked off their jobs.[26] They say that they are waiting for some foreign dignitary who has promised to take them to a much better economic environment."[27]

The city has asked for a budgetary increase to meet this potential need should the hopes of these workers prove in vain.[28]

Political Section

Last night a disturbance broke out between two religious groups, resulting in one fatality.

The news of unrest in Berea has triggered yet another political/religious confrontation here in Thessalonica.[29] The religious meetings being held in the district of Macedonia by Paul of Tarsus have taken on all the flavor of a holy war.

Can one safely mix religion and politics? Not according to a vocal group of Jewish merchants and holy men. To prove their point, they picketed an outdoor rally sponsored by this new religious cult, the Christians. A shouting match soon digressed into physical violence, and the ensuing riot left one dead. The fatality was an elderly woman who was a supporter of Paul's crusades.

A close friend of the woman said, "Sister Julia was a dear saint, and her death was a senseless act. Worst of all, she won't be here to see our Jesus when he returns."[30]

An injunction to ban future meetings of this kind was issued earlier today. A trade merchant named Jason, who figured prominently in last month's riot, has been held for arraignment.

Jason said, "None of this is our fault. The authorities have mishandled this affair from the start.[31] An innocent woman has been killed, and I have been dragged out of my house by a mob." Obviously upset and frustrated, he continued, "Who do the authorities think are the injured parties around here? Whatever happened to Roman justice?"[32]

The authorities are not very hopeful of an early end to the problem. One official said, "I wish there were some truth to this business about their god coming to take them away. It would certainly make my job a lot easier."

40

NOTE TO THE READER:

Paul's concern for an infant church, spawned in the middle of persecution, prompted him to send Timothy back to Thessalonica for firsthand news of their condition.[33] Exactly how the local news media carried the accounts of revivals and riots that followed Paul's ministry is anybody's guess.

But Paul's letter of encouragement and instruction has survived intact, carrying with it the basis for hope. Paul had planted a church in the midst of constant persecution. The survival of the church would rest largely on the source of motivation given to it at its inception. The great motivators of the world are fear, anger and guilt. But the great motivator of the Christian world is hope, grounded in love. The hope of the Second Coming[34] is the motivation Paul chose to instill in the Thessalonian church to see it through its trial.

What motivates you?

See **Garimus' Guide for Getting in Step with the Footnotes,**

which appears on page 6.

FOOTNOTES

1. Paul visited Thessalonica on his second missionary journey around A.D. 51.
2. Thessalonica was a city with a population of perhaps 200,000 (Acts 17:1).
3. Acts 17:1, 2.
4. Acts 17:4.
5. Dr. John Hannah's New Testament Survey Notes, Dallas Theological Seminary.
6. 1 Thessalonians 1:10.
7. 1 Thessalonians 4:17.
8. Acts 16:26.
9. Acts 17:5.
10. Acts 17:7.
11. Acts 17:5.

12. Acts 17:9.
13. Acts 17:5.
14. 1 Thessalonians 1:5.
15. Acts 17:2.
16. 1 Thessalonians 2:7.
17. 1 Thessalonians 2:8.
18. 1 Thessalonians 1:3; 3:6.
19. 1 Thessalonians 5:1,2.
20. Acts 17:9.
21. 1 Thessalonians 2:14.
22. Acts 17:4.
23. Acts 16:23.
24. Acts 17:10.
25. 1 Thessalonians 1:1 and Acts 17:10.
26. 1 Thessalonians 4:11.
27. 1 Thessalonians 4:17.
28. 1 Thessalonians 4:12.
29. Acts 17:13.
30. 1 Thessalonians 4:13-14.
31. 1 Thessalonians 5:12-14.

32. 1 Thessalonians 2:14; 5:14.
33. 1 Thessalonians 3:1-2.
34. 1 Thessalonians 2:19.

6
Annual Conventions and Potluck Suppers

The annual convention is as much a part of church history as fried chicken is a part of a Sunday picnic. From the Jerusalem Council to the Council of Nicea, gatherings of the church's leadership played a crucial role in the clarification and consensus of biblical doctrine and church policy.

We have the summary reports of many historical church conventions. Acts 15:23-29 is the written report of the Jerusalem Council, and the Nicean Creed marks the final products of the Council of Nicea. Is it all that unlikely that one of the New Testament letters was prompted by a similar convention?

Paul's epistle to the Ephesians is conspicuous in its focus on the church and what that is to entail. What events led up to Paul's penning the authoritative document on the church's role as the body of Christ? It wouldn't be surprising for Paul to have received an invitation to speak at a church convention in, say, Ephesus. And if he was unable to attend at that time because of his imprisonment in Rome,[1] who is to say he didn't write some sort of letter stating what he thought were the important issues of the day?[2] Of course, it would be nice if the secretary of that particular convention had requested such a document, and even nicer if we had a copy of his request.

**EPHESIAN
CONFERENCE
OF
CHRISTIAN
CHURCHES**

Dear Paul,

We are so disappointed that you will not be able to speak at the Seventh Annual Convention of the Ephesian Conference of Christian Churches (ECCC).[3] Who would have thought this trial business would drag on for so long? We have planned an old-fashioned time of fellowship at the convention; we've even rented old Tyrannus' school building [4] for the meeting hall. Delegates from all seven churches[5] in our conference have already preregistered. Still, it won't be the same without you.

I contacted Apollos[6] to see if he was available to speak in your absence. He said he'd be delighted and suggested that I write to get your opinion of what we ought to focus on this year. That way Apollos could plan his remarks around a similar theme. It occurred to me that it would be helpful for you to know how things are going here and what issues we are facing.

Last week we had a potluck supper with five pastors and their wives. The meal consisted of four types of fish and three bean salads—coordination isn't our forté.

Brother Lanis bent my ear for an hour and a half about his sermon series on spiritual gifts.[7] He has identified (by his reckoning) 57[8] distinct gifts in his study of the church. Lanis figures it will take a year and two months to complete the series. On the last two Sundays he plans to explain how all 57 gifts fit together and function.[9]

Pastor Euthus passed around a copy of his manual on

spiritual warfare using military paraphernalia as a picture of each element. He says he got the idea from one of your sermons, although he has forgotten your specific examples.

I thought you might find it revealing to see how your homiletical idea has evolved. Brother Euthus has postulated some intriguing associations: the "sword of bold action"[10]; the "helmet of good thoughts"[11]; the "girdle of self-control"[12]; and many more. Frankly, I'm afraid he is forcing his analogy to walk on all fours, and it may well roll over and play dead. What exactly *did* you say in that sermon?[13]

As you might expect, much of the evening's conversation centered on our families and churches.[14] After the obligatory tales of adolescent antics and parishioner pranks, the topic turned to the make-up of families and churches. As we talked, I couldn't help but think that there must be some close parallels between the two.[15]

There was one sad note in the evening. Dear brother Bodus has resigned from his church in Laodicea. From the table conversation, I gather his decision to leave was prompted by a familiar series of events. The giving at his church fell off for one quarter, and the financial burden began to dominate his thinking.[16] He began to question his ability and his usefulness in the ministry.[17] It has caused him to doubt his calling.[18] I fear the whole basis for the church[19] is now up for review in Bodus' mind. As wonderful as the ministry is, it isn't hard to put myself in his place. Bodus, his family, and his church greatly need our prayers[20] and the inner confidence given only from above.

Paul, you have schooled us well in the basis of our salvation.[21] What I'd like to know now is the basis of the church and its role in God's master plan.[22] I think if our church could add that knowledge to its beginning faith and love, we'd be ready to rip this place apart.

Oh yes, I should tell you too that what seems to have happened in the past is a sort of promotional approach to progress. It appears that the greatest amount of enthusiasm and commitment is found at the front end of a project. So, rather than attempt to sustain momentum, there is a tendency to invent a new program when an old one begins to fade. The result is a growing skepticism about getting involved in anything new for fear it will end up like the rest of the programs. As Merc the athlete put it, "We've been running wind sprints, but now it's time to work on stamina and distance." Many of our members hit the ground running, but they seem never to have learned how to walk.[23]

Well, I'm not sure this letter was what Apollos had in mind, but this business about the role of the church is certainly a felt need. I tend to ramble when I get excited about something. That's probably why I like being a pastor.

I truly am sorry that you are still a prisoner of the Roman government. Please know that you are often in our prayers and that we always need yours. Maybe next year your schedule will allow for a visit around convention time—the invitation is still open.

49

Nordimus

Nordimus, General Secretary of the ECCC

P.S. Any chance of sending Tychicus[24] as your alternate to our conference?

NOTE TO THE READER:

The admonition to gather together as believers is still applicable today. But the emphasis for a church is almost as varied as the number of churches. Ephesians has more to say about the role of the church than any other New Testament document.

Almost everyone has an opinion on what the emphasis should be in his church. How closely does your opinion square with Paul's?

See **Garimus' Guide for Getting in Step with the Footnotes,**

which appears on page 6.

50

FOOTNOTES

1. Ephesians 3:1; 4:1; 6:20.
2. Paul's imprisonment forced him to wean the churches from his personal visits. The reflective time afforded by prison and his concern for the churches (2 Corinthians 11:28) resulted in three of Paul's four prison letters being addressed to various churches (Ephesians, Philippians and Colossians).
3. The omission of "at Ephesus" (Ephesians 1:1) from some of the ancient manuscripts has led many scholars to think that the Ephesian epistle is a general letter to all the churches around Ephesus.
4. Acts 19:9.
5. The seven churches mentioned in Revelation 2:1—3:22 are all located in the vicinity of Ephesus and would have made good candidates for an Ephesian Conference for Christian Churches (at least in their earlier years).
6. Apollos was a man mighty in the Scriptures who seems to be just below the surface of several New Testament books (some think he may have even been the author of Hebrews). Apollos is mentioned in Acts 18:24-28; 19:1; 1 Corinthians 1:12; 3:6,21-23; 4:6; 16:12; and Titus 3:13.
7. Ephesians 4:7-13.
8. The number 57 was contrived by a famous catsup company.
9. Ephesians 4:12.

10. Ephesians 6:17.
11. *Ibid.*
12. Ephesians 6:14.
13. Ephesians 6:10-20.
14. Ephesians 5:22—6:9.
15. Ephesians 5:24-33.
16. Ephesians 1:18; 3:16.
17. Ephesians 1:19; 3:16.
18. Ephesians 1:18.
19. Ephesians 2:11-22.
20. Two of Paul's most beautiful prayers are prayed for the Church (Ephesians 1:15-23; 3:14-21).
21. Ephesians 2:1-10.
22. Ephesians 5:1-2.
23. Paul has a lot to say about walking in the Christian life (Ephesians 2:2, 10; 4:1-3, 17; 5:2, 8, 15).
24. Ephesians 6:21.

7
Do Not Pass Go

Everyone likes to get a sympathy card when things aren't going well; Paul was no exception. The church at Philippi was quick to respond to Paul's imprisonment in Rome; they sent Epaphroditus to Rome along with a financial gift for Paul's defense and housing. There's no reason to think that a sympathy card would not have followed their gift. It might even have looked a lot like this one. (Well, maybe not a lot.)

55

Dear Paul,
   We're all praying for you.[1]
                    Ambrose

P.S. The card wasn't my idea.

Dear Paul,
   Tychicus told us of your bold stand for the gospel.[2] We are as proud of you as we are of our own Roman citizenship.[3]
                    James

GET OUT OF PRISON FREE...

This card may be bartered away or used at any time.

Dear Paul,
   Our gift is for your defense and housing outside of the Mamertine[4] Prison in Rome. Demetrius, the legionnaire, has told us horror stories about that place. For our peace of mind please use the money[5] for the purpose it was intended.
                    love,
                    Cyril

Dear Paul,
   How goes your defense?[6] Things here are pretty good, but Euodia needs your prayers to help her with the humility she desperately needs.[7]
                Syntyche[8]

Dear Paul,

As always, you are frequently the topic of conversation around here. I must confess to a bit of apprehension when Dr. Luke rejoined you four years ago. [10] I wondered if we'd find ourselves meeting in my house again, [11] but PTL, the saints' participation in the gospel [12] continues with miraculous results. We all love you and long for word from you on your trial and the health of our dear Epaphroditus. [13]

Lydia [14]

Dear Paul,

Last week Deacon Hermes was arrested for just talking to some slaves in the marketplace about our fellowship in Lydia's house. [15] I went down to visit with Herm. and we had a good time of prayer and praise. You can still see the old cracks in the prison walls from the earthquake 10 years ago. Of course, I'm sure you remember that one. [16] I always will!

Julius
(your old jailer) [17]

Paul,

Last week another slave girl invited Jesus into her heart. I'm going to follow her up down near the river where you set my spirit free. [18] The last I heard, Cassandra (do you remember her?) had been sold to Caesar's household. She became a dear friend while we served our common master. Perhaps you can send her greetings from me. [19]

Althea, a slave of The Master

Dear Paul,

I wish you were here. I'm sure you'd know what to say to the "learned men of the Law." They have become a real pain in the neck, and I always come away confused and feeling inadequate. They're troubling others, too. You once summed up our worth in Christ so beautifully. Would you mind writing it to us again? [20] I think we lost the letter. [21]

Philip

Dear Paul,

It must be awfully hard to trust God over there in a Roman jail. I know I could never speak out boldly like you. Aren't you afraid of what they might think—and do? [9] I sure would be.

Timaeus

57

Dear Paul,
    We all pray that you will soon be released. As I'm sure you remember, I was to lead our time of fellowship and prayer among the women, but I'm getting some opposition. Don't worry, though. I'll see to it that the prayers continue.
                                                            Euodia[22]

Dear Paul,
    How are you? Word has reached us that our dear brother Epaphroditus is very sick.[23] We're praying continuallly for both your releases from your various bondages. Oh yes, a word from you concerning true humility[24] could help to clear up a divisive conflict between two of our dear sisters.[25] Thanks a lot.
                                                            Your comrade,
                                                            Syzygus[26]

Dear Paul,
    The church here at Philippi[27] continues to grow amidst increasing opposition.[28] Our joy would be complete if only you could be with us.[29] You are loved and missed in Philippi, the little Rome of Macedonia.
                                                            Clement, the overseer[30]

NOTE TO THE READER:

Paul had started the church at Philippi with a cloth merchant, a slave girl, and the town jailer (Acts 16:14-40). A special collection for saints. On three previous occasions they had sent him a gift (twice while he was in Thessalonica[31], and once while he was in Corinth[32]), and now, over 10 years later, their love and generosity were manifested again. The apostle Paul had left the infant church in the care of Luke amid a teeming Roman colony of more than a quarter of a million people. This was to be the first of many European churches, and it held a special place in the apostle's heart. It is no wonder that his thank you note is so full of joy and love.

When was the last time you wrote an encouraging note to your favorite missionary? Don't have one? Well...[33]

See **Garimus' Guide for Getting in Step with the Footnotes,**

which appears on page 6.

59

FOOTNOTES

1. Philippians 1:19.
2. Philippians 1:12-13, 26.
3. The Philippians boasted of their Roman citizenship (Acts 16:20-21), but Paul reminded them of their more important citizenship in heaven (Philippians 3:20).
4. Mamertine Prison is a small prison still preserved in the center of Rome. According to tradition, Paul was imprisoned there. See *Oxford Dictionary of the Christian Church,* by F. L. Cross and Elizabeth A. Livingstone, NY: Oxford University Press, 1974, p. 863.
5. Philippians 4:18.
6. Philippians 1:7.
7. Philippians 2 exhorts them to true humility, giving four examples : Christ (vv. 5-11); Paul (vv. 12-18); Timothy (vv. 19-24); and their own Epaphroditus (vv. 25-30).

8. Philippians 4:2 records a problem between these two women. Some scholars feel that their differences centered on the issue of humility.

9. Philippians 1-27-30 gives Paul's outlook on opposition.

10. A comparison of the first-person accounts of Acts 16:10-13 and the omission of any first-person pronouns until Acts 20:5 (the beginning of Paul's third missionary journey) have led scholars to believe that Luke stayed on in Philippi to pastor the church for six years.

11. Acts 16:14-15.

12. Philippians 1:5.

13. Philippians 2:25-30. Epaphroditus was the church's emissary to Paul, delivering their gift in Rome. While in Rome, Epaphroditus became very sick.

14. Acts 16:14.

15. Philippians 1:29-30.

16. Acts 16:23-28.

17. Acts 16:23-34.

18. Acts 16:16-18.

19. Philippians 4:22.

20. Philippians 3 is Paul's great contrast between the world's idea of success and true success in Christ.

21. Philippians 3:1.

22. Philippians 4:2.

23. Philippians 2:26.

24. Philippians 2.

25. Philippians 4:2.

26. Philippians 4:3. "True comrade" is a translation of the Greek name *Syzygus.*

27. Philippians 1:1.

28. Philippians 1:29-30.

29. Philippians 1:25.

30. Philippians 4:3.

31. Philippians 4:15-16.

32. 2 Corinthians 11:9.

33. Feel free to send any notes and gifts to: Garimus, Here's Life Publishers, P.O. Box 1576, San Bernardino, CA 92402.

8
No Deposit, No Return

The letter to Philemon is all that remains of Paul's efforts to help one of his converts get his life straightened out. Onesimus was a slave.[1] He ran away from Philemon,[2] his master; made his way to Rome; and became a Christian after meeting Paul[3]. On the eve of Paul's trial before Caesar and with the press of the churches on him,[4] Paul still found time to compose a brief note on behalf of Onesimus. That Paul should write such a note isn't the least bit odd. But that a note written to an obscure individual from a town Paul never visited[5] should find a place among the rest of the New Testament—that's another matter.

Perhaps the theme of Paul's little note is the reason for its popularity; it touches a universal need—forgiveness. In the 25 verses of Philemon, Paul relates six basic elements of forgiveness[6] to Onesimus and Philemon. But how the note to Philemon was written in the first place. . .well, the following scraps of correspondence (real or otherwise) may unlock some doors.

Dear Onesimus,

A pastor friend of mine named Epaphras[7] arrived yesterday from Colossae. As I was telling Epaphras about you and how useful[8] you have been to me since our first meeting, he expressed surprise. It seems that Philemon, a believer from Colossae, once had a slave by the same name.[9] Onesimus is a common enough name (especially among slaves), but from what Epaphras tells me, you two could be twins! It's a small world, isn't it, Onesimus?

Your brother,
Paul

Dear Paul,

It was just a matter of time before I was found out. Well, I'm kinda relieved. Epaphras has been to my master's house lots—that's where their church meets.[10] I wasn't bothered at all by my actions until I met you and then God. But now I'm sorry I ran away[11] (not to mention the stealing).[12] I've tried to forget it all and work on doing better now. It hasn't helped much. I thought Christians was supposed to feel forgiven.

Your servant,
Onesimus

Dear Onesimus,

You're right; a letter is a good idea. I'll gladly write him a note explaining the situation and interceding on your behalf. But forgiveness simply won't work in the abstract. Its sweet savor is only found when it's done face-to-face;[20] I know.[21] I want you to stay, but you need to go back. I'll write the letter—but then you deliver it.[22]

Love,
Paul, the Apostle

68

NOTE TO THE READER:

Onesimus did deliver Paul's note, and Philemon did forgive him. Tradition[23] holds that Philemon sent Onesimus back to Rome to serve Paul. More than 50 years later, a man named Onesimus was the bishop of the church at Ephesus, probably the first place an effort was made to collect the books of our New Testament. If Onesimus was indeed the bishop during that time, how appropriate that he would want a little note on a grand theme to be included.

Many sides of forgiveness are found in Paul's note to Philemon. See if you can find the six steps Paul took in the case of Onesimus. Can you parallel Paul's handling of this specific case with Christ's efforts on your behalf?

"No deposit, no return" is found on things society deems of no worth once they are used up. Paul was unfamiliar with this phrase, much to Onesimus' good fortune.

There is a phrase that at least one modest scholar thinks Paul was familiar with—"To redeem, return to maker."

69

See **Garimus' Guide for Getting in Step with the Footnotes,**

which appears on page 6.

FOOTNOTES

1. Philemon 16.
2. Philemon 11.
3. Philemon 10.
4. Ephesians, Philippians, and Colossians all were written from prison by Paul about the same time as Philemon (A.D. 62).
5. Colossians 1:4, 8.
6. 1) The offense; 2) Compassion; 3) Intercession; 4) Substitution; 5) Restoration to favor; and 6) A new relationship. Merrill Tenney, *New Testament Survey*, Grand Rapids, Mich.: Wm. B. Eerdmans Publishing Co., 1961, p. 317.

7. Epaphras was likely the pastor in Colossae (Colossians 4:12-13), and he went to Rome to help Paul during his time of need (Philemon 23). Epaphras also prompted Paul to write to the church at Colossae concerning the heresies there (Colossians 1:7-8).
8. Paul is making a pun on Onesimus' name, which means "useful" (Philemon 11).
9. Philemon 10-11.
10. Philemon 2.
11. Philemon 15.
12. Philemon 18.
13. A Roman master was free to punish a runaway slave with virtually any punishment he wished, including death. For further details see William Barclay's *Letters to Timothy, Titus and Philemon,* pp. 310ff.
14. Acts 22:27-28.
15. Philemon 8, 9, 21.
16. Philemon 11.
17. Philemon 14.
18. Romans 6:17-18.
19. Philemon 13.
20. Philemon 14.
21. Acts 9 tells the story of how Paul found forgiveness on the road to Damascus.

22. Philemon 12; Colossians 4:7-9.
23. Ignatius wrote a letter to the church of Ephesus around A.D. 115, making mention of their bishop Onesimus. He even used the same pun Paul used on Onesimus' name.

72

9
Liars, Evil Beasts and Lazy Gluttons

Titus' Test (Multiple Choice)

_____ 1. When stuck in the last place on earth you want to be, you should:
   A. Put as much distance between yourself and that place as you can.
   B. Pout and complain, thereby adding to the negative aspects of the place.
   C. Carry on quietly and thus gain martyr points with which to club someone later.
   D. Write a letter to the one who put you there and point out (graciously, of course) the blunder he has made in sending you there.

_____ 2. When given a job that you don't want to do with a bunch of people you don't like, you should:
   A. Quit.
   B. Nuke them.
   C. Get it over with as quickly and painlessly as possible (remember those martyr points).
   D. Write a letter to the one who gave you the assignment and point out (graciously of course) the blunder he made in handing you that particular job.

74

The correct answer to both questions is **D** according to one of the creative sermons of Pastor Charles Blair, Denver.

—If you got any of the answers wrong, you should peruse Titus's air mail letter to Paul.

—If you got all of the answers right, you should certainly read Titus' letter to Paul. It might help you with any academic pride problems you may now need to deal with.

Dear Paul,

This is Titus, the fellow you left on the Isle of Crete to head up the church work there.[1] I have been thinking about you since your departure for Nicopolis[2] and wanted to write and wish you God's grace, mercy and peace.

Speaking of peace, there's been precious little of it around here since you left. Oh, the island is nice enough, and there is no end to the distractions the Cretans have to offer, but I'm more than a little concerned. So many things around here remind me of our times together—the riots in Thessalonica,[3] your imprisonment in Philippi,[4] and your stories about the time you were stoned in Lystra.[5]

When the islanders aren't inventing some new form of vice, they are helping the church folks excel in the old ones. If you think we had problems in Corinth, you should spend a little time on Crete. I have never seen such a group of rebellious, devious reprobates in my whole life. And those are the religious folks, Paul![6] Wait till I tell you about the rest of these islanders.

I forget who said it first, but it's true: "Cretans are always liars, evil beasts and lazy gluttons."[7] Paul, are you getting the picture? How a church comes to be here in the first place is as great a mystery as Pentecost.[8] That any church has survived in this environment staggers the imagination, and the thought of planting a church in every city is enough to bring on the palsy. The closest thing to a church leader I have found so far is an old heretic who will say anything if there's the slightest

75

chance it will turn a profit.[10] About the only unifying element in the church is the common disregard for authority, especially mine.[11]

I'm very curious to know how Timothy is faring in Ephesus;[12] it's got to be better than this. I feel I can say with great certainty that the Isle of Crete is really a synonym for the Stables of Augeas.[13]

I don't think you have a realistic picture of this place, even though you stopped here on your way to Rome for an audience with Caesar.[14] Perhaps if you had been allowed to move about freely during your brief visit, you would have seen what Crete is really like. Let's face it — you arrived on Crete in a prison ship.[15] Wouldn't any place named "Fair Havens"[16] conjure up visions of peace and rest? I can tell you from firsthand experience that the island's naming of such places shows a considerable lack of insight.

This may be coming across as a bit critical, but I think of it as discernment of the highest order. What I'm trying to say is this: I feel certain that a placement error has been made, and I want to give you this opportunity to right the mistake. It boggles the imagination to think that I've taken up residence here. The Second Coming can't come soon enough!

Now that I've got my frustrations down on paper, I want you to know that I am not a quitter. I did not quit when you sent me to Corinth to raise funds.[17] I did not quit when you suggested that I accompany you and Barnabas to Jerusalem, even though there was no small risk to my person.[18] But, in the whole of our 15-year association,[19] Crete has got to be the hardest to take. I will stay on in Crete until you say I can go, but that can't be soon enough.

In the midst of all these problems, I can't even remember why I'm here. You always seem to have a reason for what you do,[20] so would you mind terribly refreshing my memory?[21] It was so much easier to take up the challenge when I could see a chance of success.[22]

I can just see that knowing little smile of yours as you are reading this. I get the funny feeling you are going to tell me that all of my life I will find myself either in Crete or on my way to Crete. Paul, I really don't want to hear that. But like I said earlier, I am willing to stay. It's the least I can do in light of our Lord's willingness to stay under far more desperate circumstances.[23] He always shines brightest on our "Isles of Crete," doesn't He?

Of course, Paul, I am *still* prepared to drop everything at once and join you in Nicopolis; you have only to say the word. In the meantime, could you send any help my way?[24] I also heard a rumor that Apollos and Zenas, the lawyer (who would find no lack of work on this rock), might be coming this way.[25] Is there anything special you would like me to do for them while I'm still here? I look forward to hearing from you very soon.

Sincerely and expectantly yours,

Titus

Note to the Reader:

Titus did eventually visit Paul in Nicopolis and even went on to Dalmatia.[26] But tradition holds that Titus went back to Crete to oversee the churches there until he was very old.[27]

Of course, Titus' situation is a common experience for us all. What is your "Isle of Crete"? Perhaps you ought to construct a letter, too, for you are bound to spend some time there.

See **Garimus' Guide for Getting in Step with the Footnotes,**

which appears on page 6.

FOOTNOTES

1. Titus 1:4, 5.
2. Titus 3:12.
3. Acts 17:8.
4. Acts 16:23.
5. Acts 14:19.
6. Titus 1:10.
7. Titus 1:12.
8. Acts 2:11.
9. Titus 1:5.
10. Titus 1:11.
11. Titus 2:15.
12. 1 Timothy 1:3.
13. Myth says that King Augeas kept three thousand oxen in his stables, which were uncleaned for 30 years until Hercules was given the task.
14. Acts 25:11.
15. Acts 27:1.
16. Acts 27:8.
17. 2 Corinthians 8:6.
18. Galatians 2:1.

19. Galatians was Paul's first letter, written about A.D. 49. Titus was one of Paul's last letters, written about A.D. 65.
20. Ephesians 3:1; 2 Timothy 2:10.
21. Titus 1:5.
22. 2 Corinthians 8:17; Titus 2:7.
23. John 12:27.
24. Titus 3:12.
25. Titus 3:13.
26. 2 Timothy 4:10.
27. Eusebius, *Historia Ecclesiastria,* iii 4.6.

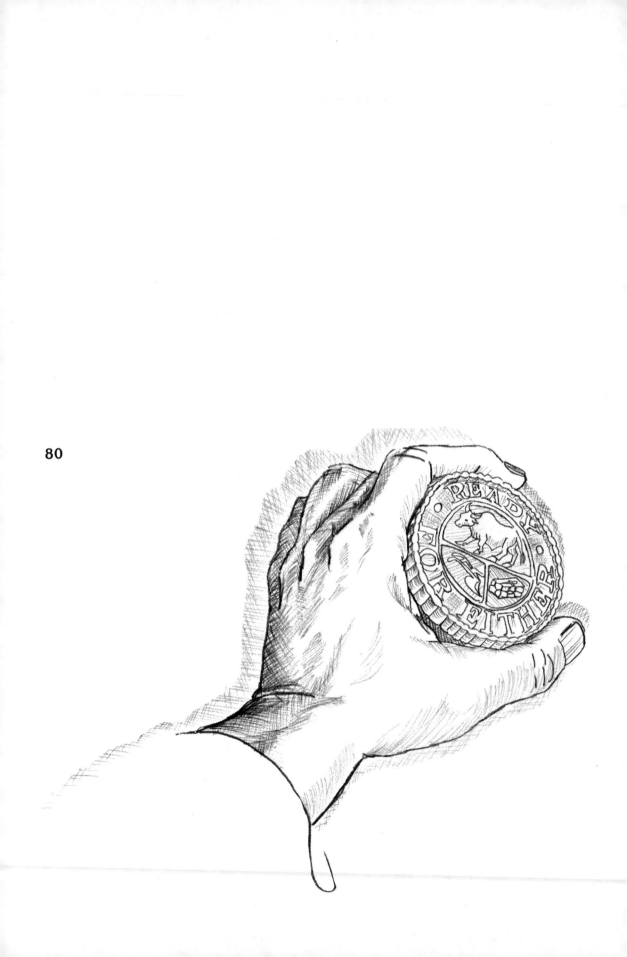

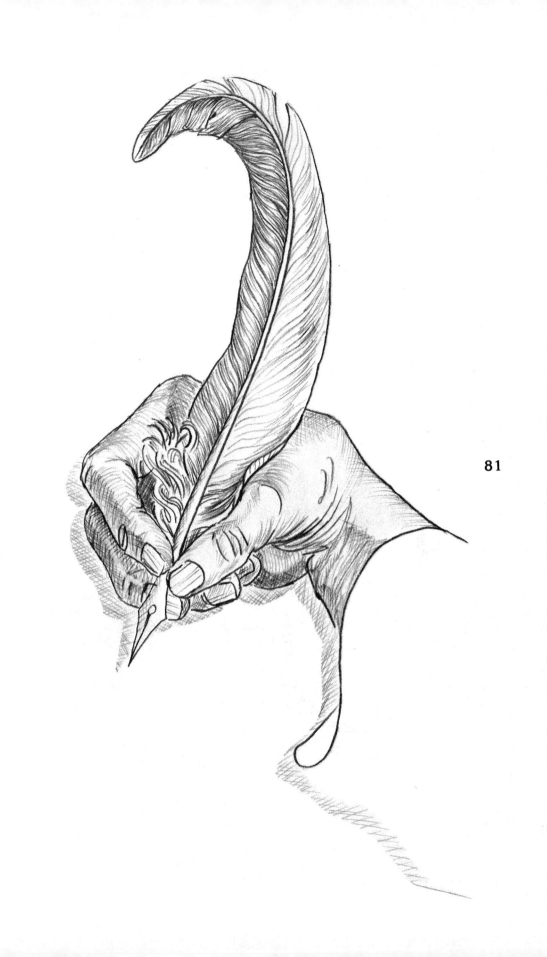

81

10
The Legacy of a Dream

In one form or another, diaries have been around at least since the days when David penned his Psalms. Parts of Acts most likely originated in Luke's travel diary. But most diaries are a quiet reflection written to oneself, a private record of the dreams and fears surrounding the turning points of life.

Timothy was in his thirties when he received Paul's last letter (2 Timothy), urging him to come to Rome. For half a lifetime Paul was the guiding influence in Timothy's life.[1] And now Paul's imprisonment in Rome was about to be ended with his execution.[2]

How did Timothy react to the letter? How does anyone deal with the loss of the central personality in one's life? Maybe, just maybe, the entries in Timothy's diary read something like this:

Dear Diary,

    A letter arrived today from Paul.[3] It came much too soon; I'm not ready. Paul may finally give up his life for the gospel.[4]

    For six years he's been ready to go home,[5] and it's selfish to wish him with me always, but I do. I'm scared to death that I won't be able to live out his dream. He sees the whole purpose of life so clearly,[6] and I stumble at every turn. Oh God, help me not to fall short like so many others![7]

    It doesn't sound like Paul has much time left.[8] I so want to say goodbye one more time. Next to my Heavenly Father, no one has made such a difference in me as that man.[9] Please let there be time.

    . . . Calm down, Timothy, quiet your soul and seek His face. John Mark must be notified immediately,[10] travel money must be collected, and arrangements for the care of the church must be made (Paul would send me packing if I failed to provide for the church).[11] No need to plan a travel itinerary; Paul has taken care of that.[12] (He always likes to lead, even from prison.) I need to take along some warm clothes. There may not be time for all of this!

    Timothy, you can't be responsible for everything. Do what you can and depend on His grace.[13] God remains faithful; for He cannot deny Himself.[14]

    I've been wrapped up in Paul's dream for close to 18 years, and good bye or not, it's my turn to lead. I'll get there as fast as I can . . .

Dear Diary,

It's only been a week. I've relived each detail until I'm numb. The crowds, the soldiers, the insanity of it all. Standing at the edge of the crowd, I prayed that God would do something at the last moment to prevent this awful wrong. Maybe He did, but I didn't see it. For a week now, all I've been able to see is a sword fall, and Paul's earthly life end.

But when a saint dies, there's more to it than just the tears.[15] I keep thinking of Paul's last letter, which brought me to Rome. "Timothy, remember your heritage.[16] Timothy, remember your calling.[17] Timothy, preach the word.[18] Timothy, exercise your gift.[19] Timothy, come to me soon."[20] The list goes on and on.

For 18 years Paul treated me like a son. And for 18 years I lived in his world, traveling with him and going wherever he sent me.[21] It seemed to me that his dream was big enough to encompass a world,[22] but can it survive without him?

. . . That was the purpose of the letter, wasn't it? He didn't pass on a list of do's and don'ts; he gave me his dream. He meant me to be his living legacy.

I'm willing to pursue the dream he cherished for a lifetime. Oh, Father, help me to finish the course, too![23]

. . . But what now? Do I stay and embrace the same fate as Paul, or do I escape for a season? Peter fled the city earlier this week, but he came back determined to face it all.[24] Talk on the street is that Nero has a cross waiting for him.[25]

I keep thinking of the Roman coin Paul gave me with its engraved ox staring at a plow and an altar. The inscription, "Ready for either," 26 is almost worn away. When is the right time for martyrdom? How often Paul must have faced that same question. It's not really my decision, is it? Like Paul, I will strive to live out the dream as long as God lets me. And when it's time, I pray that He will grant me the grace to embrace death the way Paul did—a homecoming after a long journey.

NOTE TO THE READER:

The biblical account mentions Timothy only once after Paul's death.[27] The implication is that Timothy was imprisoned but did not die with Paul and Peter in Rome. Tradition holds that Timothy picked up the dream and went on to become the bishop of Ephesus and years later was martyred during Domitian's reign (81-96). He took both the plow and the altar.

My own diary isn't a daily discipline, but when I walk back through its pages, I find God's grace waiting for me. More than that, I'm reminded of the investments made in my life and the dreams that prompted them.

Perhaps not everyone needs to keep a journal or a diary, but everyone does need the memory of what others have invested in them. Paul is so careful in his letter to lay out all the investments made in Timothy, and then Paul calls for him to take his place as a living legacy of his dream of bringing the gospel to the whole world.

If Paul were writing this letter to you, what investments in your life would he mention? And what investments can you make in someone else's life to place him or her in the tradition of 2 Timothy 2:2: "And the things which you have heard from me in the presence of many witnesses, these entrust to faithful men, who will be able to teach others also."

86

See **Garimus' Guide for Getting in Step with the Footnotes,**

which appears on page 6.

FOOTNOTES

1. Timothy probably met Paul during Paul's first missionary journey (Acts 14:6-26) around A.D. 48. During the second missionary journey, Paul took Timothy with him (Acts 16:1—18:22). Seventeen years later, Timothy was still considered a youth (1 Timothy 4:12), and by the writing of 2 Timothy A.D. 67, Timothy was probably about 30.
2. Tradition holds that Paul was executed in Rome by the sword during Nero's reign.
3. 2 Timothy.

4. 2 Timothy 4:6.
5. Philippians 1:23.
6. Galatians 1:16; 1 Timothy 2:7.
7. 2 Timothy 4:16.
8. 2 Timothy 4:6.
9. 2 Timothy 1:2.
10. 2 Timothy 4:11.
11. 1 Timothy 3:15.
12. 2 Timothy 4:13.
13. 2 Timothy 2:1.
14. 2 Timothy 2:13.
15. 2 Timothy 4:8; Philippians 3:20.
16. 2 Timothy 1:5.
17. 2 Timothy 1:9.
18. 2 Timothy 4:2.
19. 2 Timothy 1:6.
20. 2 Timothy 4:9,21.
21. See note 1.
22. 2 Corinthians 5:18-19; 2 Timothy 2:2.
23. 2 Timothy 4:7.
24. Tradition states that Peter was escaping from Rome when he met the risen Lord. Peter asked Jesus, "Quo vadis?" ("Where are you going?") Jesus replied that He was going to Rome to die in Peter's place. In response, Peter went back, unwilling to deny his Lord a second time. See William Barclay, *The Master's Men* (Nashville: Abingdon, 1959), p. 26.
25. Tradition also claims that Peter was crucified upside down in Rome. See Barclay, p. 27.
26. *Ibid.,* p. 104.
27. Hebrews 13:23.

88

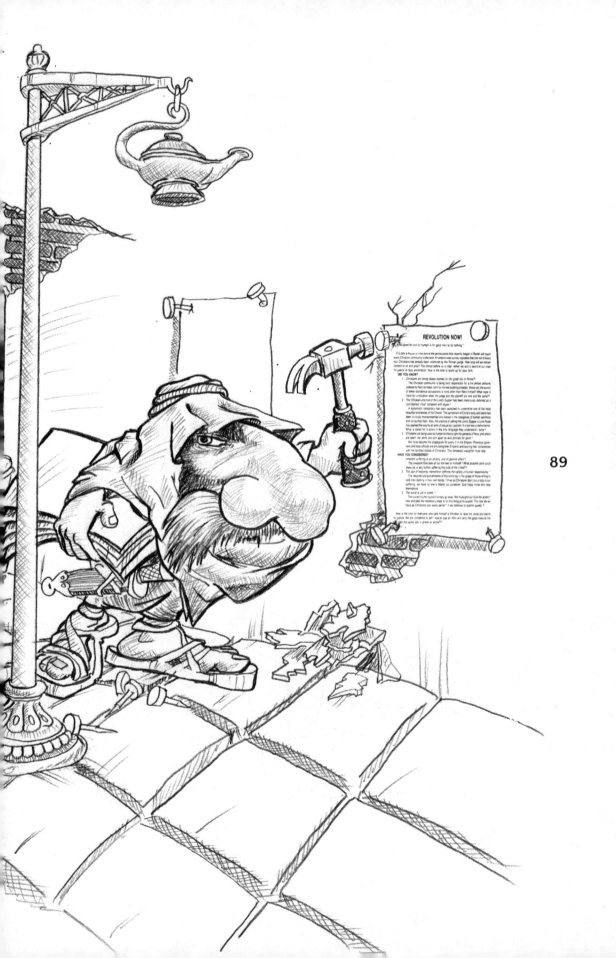

89

11
Tracts of a Fellow Sufferer

Pamphleteering has long been an effective tool in stirring the masses to action in troubled times. In 1848, Karl Marx published his Communist Manifesto, laying the groundwork for a movement that would shadow two-thirds of the world. Nearly a hundred years previous, Thomas Paine's "Common Sense" (published in 1776) helped spark the American Revolution. And more than 250 years earlier, the tracts of Martin Luther fueled the fires of reformation in Germany.

Who's to say that other pamphlets didn't surface in the Roman world during the persecutions of Christians under Nero? These pamphlets may well have carried a cry for armed revolution. Perhaps the following tract (found in an overdue library book) prompted Peter to write a persuasive letter of his own.

REVOLUTION NOW!

"All it takes for evil to triumph is for good men to do nothing."[1]

It is only a matter of time before the persecutions that recently began in Rome[2] will touch every Christian community in the land. An empire-wide survey indicates that one out of every four Christians has already been victimized by this Roman purge. How long will we remain content to sit and pray? The choice before us is clear: either we add a sword to our cries for justice or face annihilation. Now is the time to stand up for your faith.

DID YOU KNOW?

1. *Christians are being falsely blamed for the great fire of Rome?*[3]

   The Christian community is being held responsible for a fire almost certainly ordered by Nero (to make room for his new building projects). Worse yet, the source of these slanderous accusations is none other than Nero himself! What hope is there for vindication when the judge and the plaintiff are one and the same?[4]

2. *The Christian practice of the Lord's Supper has been maliciously defamed as a cannibalistic ritual, complete with orgies.*[5]

   A systematic conspiracy has been launched to undermine one of the most beautiful ordinances of the Church. The symbolism of Christ's body and blood has been viciously misrepresented and placed in the categories of human sacrifices and consumed flesh. Also, the practice of calling the Lord's Supper a Love Feast has opened the way for all sorts of sexual accusations. It is too late to define terms. What is called for is action in the only language they understand—force.[6]

3. *Christians are being used as human torches to light the gardens of Nero, and others are sewn into skins and torn apart by wild animals for sport.*[7]

   We have become the scapegoats for every ill in the Empire. Provincial governors and local officials are emulating their Emperor and searing their consciences with the torched bodies of Christians. This senseless slaughter must stop.

HAVE YOU CONSIDERED?

I. *Innocent suffering is an atrocity void of positive effect.*[8]

   The innocent One took all our sorrows on Himself.[9] What possible point could there be in any further suffering this side of the cross?[10]

2. *The lack of heavenly intervention confirms the validity of human responsibility.*[11]

   The rewards and punishments of this world lay in the grasp of those willing to take their destiny in their own hands.[12] If we as Christians don't put a stop to our suffering, we have no one to blame but ourselves. God helps those who help themselves.

3. *The worst is yet to come.*[13]

   The current suffering won't simply go away. We must gird our loins for action[14] now and take the necessary steps to kill this thing at its source. The new life we have as Christians can easily perish[15] if we continue to submit quietly.[16]

Now is the time for everyone who calls himself a Christian to raise his voice and sword for justice. We are compelled to act[17] now or lose all. Who will carry the good news to the lost if all the saved are in prison or worse?[18]

NOTE TO THE READER:

At first glance, the preceding revolutionary pamphlet might sound like something a young Peter would have handed out on a street corner. A more volatile and impulsive Christian would be hard to find in the first-century world. After all, wasn't it Peter who sliced off an enemy's ear[19] and boasted of standing up to the authorities?[20] And didn't Peter rebuke Jesus for His willingness to accept death at the hands of their enemies?[21] It was Peter, wasn't it, who said, "We must obey God rather than men,"[22] and later escaped from jail?[23] Anyone impulsive enough to jump out of a boat and walk on water[24] isn't likely to endure persecution patiently.

However, the Peter we find penning advice to some fellow sufferers takes a radically different stance. Peter's counsel goes so much against his old human nature that it's hard to believe he is the same man. He isn't. After 30 years of service to his Lord, Peter has a whole new perspective on the proper attitude one should have when confronted with suffering.[25]

Peter's position isn't merely the passive acceptance of persecution that the author of the revolutionary pamphlet might think. In fact, Peter's final exhortation may take you by surprise, "Stand firm in the true grace of God!"[26]

How well do you handle unjust suffering? Yeah, me too. But if Peter can change, there's hope for us. I wonder how he did it.[27]

92

See **Garimus' Guide for Getting in Step with the Footnotes,**

which appears on page 6.

FOOTNOTES

1. The quote is from Edmond Burke and sounds very much like Romans 12:21. Any quote, however, taken out of context, can be used to enhance virtually any argument.
2. On July 19, A.D. 64, there was a fire in Rome, and the Christians were a convenient group on which to place the blame.
3. Tacitus, *Annals,* NY: St. Martins Press, Inc., 1959, 15:44.
4. 1 Peter 1:3,21.

5. William Barclay, *Letters of James and Peter,* Edinburgh, Scotland: The Saint Andrew Press, 1973, p. 175.

6. 1 Peter 2:12; 3:8-9; 4:15.

7. Tacitus, *Annals,* 15:44.

8. 1 Peter 2:19-20.

9. 1 Peter 3:18.

10. 1 Peter 2:21; 4:1.

11. 1 Peter 5:6-7.

12. 1 Peter 4:19.

13. 1 Peter 5:10.

14. 1 Peter 1:13.

15. 1 Peter 1:23.

16. 1 Peter 2:16.

17. 1 Peter 5:2.

18. 1 Peter 3:15.

19. John 18:10.

20. Luke 22:38.

21. Matthew 16:22.

22. Acts 5:29.

23. Acts 12:6.

24. Matthew 14:28.

25. Three of Peter's suggestions are found in 1 Peter 1:7,13; 2:20-24; 4:13; and 5:10. Peter also found three rare values in suffering properly borne (1 Peter 3:13-16; 3:17-22; and 4:1-11). See Walter Dunnett, *An Outline of New Testament Survey*, Chicago: Moody Press, 1960, p. 150.

26. 1 Peter 5:12.

27. If you still think Peter got his act together on his own, you have missed much more than you know. See 1 Peter 5:10.

12
Empire Dispatch Service

It is amazing how much can be said in a few words. Jesus summed up the Law and the Prophets in only two sentences (Matthew 22:37,39). One of the most effective prayers ever prayed was just three words long (Matthew 14:30). And many of the letters of the New Testament take only a few minutes to read.

The letters of 2 Peter and Jude are prime examples of "good things in small packages." The similarities between these two letter strongly suggest some form of collaboration.[1] What if their written interaction was done in the classic form of brevity—the telegram.

Perhaps some enterprising (and energetic) young Romans had started such a public messenger service. For so much a word and so much a mile they would deliver any message anywhere in the empire. They might even call their business the Empire Dispatch Service.

If such a thing had existed, Peter might well have availed himself of their service when confronted with the gravest danger the church would ever face...

Empire Dispatch Service

"WE DELIVER"
"From Rome To The Empire In Three Months Or Less"

DATE: OCT 12 A.D. 67

TO: JUDE BEN JOSEPH[2]
       412 COLONNADES WAY
       ANTIOCH, SYRIA

MESSAGE: HOW THINGS ANTIOCH?[3] STOP ROME
              DANGEROUS[4] STOP HEARD RUMORS
              HERESIES IN ASIA MINOR CHURCHES[5]
              STOP ANY NEWS? STOP GOOD LUCK
              ON TREATISE[6] STOP ENJOYED PAST
              TRIADS[7] STOP PETER

Empire Dispatch Service

"WE DELIVER"
"From Rome To The Empire In Three Months Or Less"

DATE: OCT 27 A.D. 67

TO: JUDE BEN JOSEPH
         412 COLONNADES WAY
         ANTIOCH, SYRIA

MESSAGE: RUMORS CONFIRMED STOP REMEMBER
           WORDS OF APOSTLES[8] STOP TROUBLE
           FROM WITHIN THIS TIME STOP HARD
           TO BELIEVE AFTER RECENT EVENTS[9]
           STOP PLAN SECOND LETTER[10] STOP
           MORE LATER STOP PRAY NOW STOP
           PETER

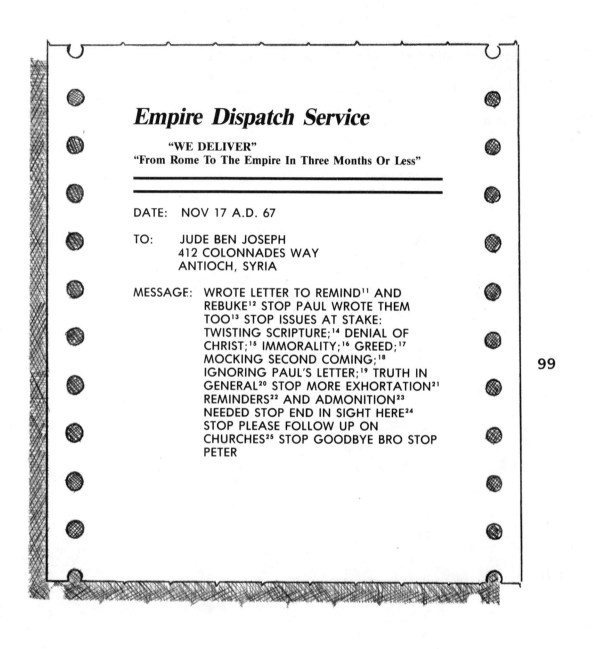

Empire Dispatch Service

"WE DELIVER"
"From Rome To The Empire In Three Months Or Less"

DATE: NOV 17 A.D. 67

TO: JUDE BEN JOSEPH
         412 COLONNADES WAY
         ANTIOCH, SYRIA

MESSAGE: WROTE LETTER TO REMIND[11] AND
           REBUKE[12] STOP PAUL WROTE THEM
           TOO[13] STOP ISSUES AT STAKE:
           TWISTING SCRIPTURE;[14] DENIAL OF
           CHRIST;[15] IMMORALITY;[16] GREED;[17]
           MOCKING SECOND COMING;[18]
           IGNORING PAUL'S LETTER;[19] TRUTH IN
           GENERAL[20] STOP MORE EXHORTATION[21]
           REMINDERS[22] AND ADMONITION[23]
           NEEDED STOP END IN SIGHT HERE[24]
           STOP PLEASE FOLLOW UP ON
           CHURCHES[25] STOP GOODBYE BRO STOP
           PETER

99

NOTE TO THE READER:

When one's children are threatened, many responses are likely: anxiety, fear, anger, or even physical violence. (Just try stepping between a mother bear and her cub!) The early Christian leaders had a parental concern for the church, and they kept close tabs on it. That concern was never more evident than when the church was threatened with heresy from within. Instead of rushing out on their own to vanquish the enemy or summon up some kind of inquisition, the New Testament writers marshaled together to confront the danger collectively.[26]

John, Paul, Peter and Jude each wrote at least one letter to a church (or group of churches) troubled by heresy.[27] It appears that three of them addressed the same heretical situation existing in Asia Minor.

Each man refrained from calling for the death of the false teachers but left the condemnation to God's direction.[28] They chose instead to focus on Christ's utter sufficiency[29] and showed that the new threat wasn't unexpected.[30]

Peter and Jude vented the rest of their parental indignation by pointing out the consequences of such heresies in history. They conclude with the thought that God is the One who keeps us from stumbling[31] or allows us to find our own destruction.[32] The choice is ours.[33]

Heresies can sneak in a window or knock at your front door. Have you checked your locks lately?

100

See **Garimus' Guide for Getting in Step with the Footnotes,**

which appears on page 6.

FOOTNOTES

1. The similarities are remarkable. Jude 17-18 quote 2 Peter 3:3 (or vice versa). Both epistles use fallen angels, Sodom and Gomorrah, and Balaam as examples.
2. Jude was the brother of James (Jude 1) and James was the brother of Jesus, which makes Joseph Jude's father; thus the surname Ben (son of) Joseph.

3. Jude's location is just a guess.
4. Nero's Rome was volatile at best and frequently deadly for Christians.
5. The churches of Asia Minor mentioned in 1 Peter 1:1 give us the location of the heresies. Apparently 2 Peter (see 3:1) and Jude are written to the same situation. Thus it can be deduced that Jude was also addressed to the same audience.
6. Jude 3.
7. Jude is filled with triplets, beginning with his own introduction as Jude, bondservant, and brother (Jude 1).
8. Jude 17-18 and 2 Peter 3:3.
9. 1 Peter was written in response to the sufferings from persecution in Asia Minor. Apparently the dangers from without (persecutions) had been replaced with dangers from within (heresies).
10. 2 Peter 3:1.
11. 2 Peter 1:12-13; 3:2.
12. 2 Peter 2:1.
13. 2 Peter 3:15 seems to indicate that Paul had also written these believers.
14. 2 Peter 1:20-21; Jude 19.
15. 2 Peter 2:1; Jude 4.
16. 2 Peter 2:2; Jude 4, 18.
17. 2 Peter 2:3; Jude 16.
18. 2 Peter 3:3-4, 12; Jude 21.

19. 2 Peter 3:15-16.
20. It is interesting to note that Jude quotes two extrabiblical sources to drive home his point (the Assumption of Moses in verse 9, and the Book of Enoch in verse 14). Paul also quoted nonbiblical sources on occasion (Acts 17:28). The sources Jude quotes are not inspired, but they do contain some truths, two of which the Holy Spirit has chosen to endorse by having them included in the book of Jude. Remember, all truth is God's truth.
21. Jude 3-4.
22. Jude 5-16.
23. Jude 17-23.
24. 2 Peter 1:14.
25. He did, with the letter we know as the book of Jude.
26. See note 13.
27. John wrote 1 John in part to deal with the gnostic heresy, and Paul wrote Colossians to dispel several heresies.
28. 2 Peter 2:1; Jude 4.
29. 2 Peter 1:17; 3:18; Jude 24.
30. 2 Peter 3:1-4; Jude 17-18.
31. Jude 24.
32. 2 Peter 3:16.
33. 2 Peter 1:10.

13
Reasons and Rationales

What do you do when someone you care for takes a wrong turn and all your counsel and advice is ignored? You've prayed, you've cajoled, and you've pleaded, but your attempts to help don't seem to meet the person's needs. Somehow his or her reasons and rationales don't fit any familiar categories, and the standard answers no longer satisfy. If you could just talk to someone who had seen the "answers" in the making, you're sure he could demonstrate that those old answers are still trustworthy today.

At the close of the first century that person could have been the ancient Son of Thunder[1] who never got over the fact that Jesus loved him. He was the last eyewitness[2] of Christ. His name was John, and he lived in Ephesus.

Who is to say that a pastor named Gaius[3] didn't find himself a puzzled counselor and, in his desperation, turned to John, the elder statesman of the church. If so, John's first epistle might have been prompted by the following...

104

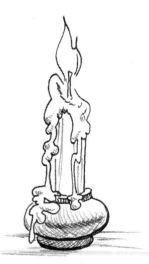

Dear John,

I should have written you sooner, but I didn't realize the importance of what was happening until yesterday. For years, a close friend of mine named Aphileo has been coming with his family to our fellowship. He has a quick mind and an eager heart and endears himself to one and all. About nine months ago, he left our church and became involved with a new group in town. They talk about "building on one's basic faith" and reaching a "higher level of maturity." On the surface that all sounds fine. After all, growth is the natural consequence of birth.

Some of our folks thought there was no harm in Aphileo's new interest. There were some differences from our church, but they seemed insignificant in comparison to the Greek and Roman religions we contend with. A few, including myself, felt that these new beliefs constituted a danger.[4] But none of us could see where the arguments of Aphileo's teacher, Cerinthus,[5] would lead. Perhaps you've heard of him; he's a very persuasive, philosophical speaker. I'm afraid my interest in the practical areas of life has kept me away from the study of current philosophy. But after a time it began to look as though Cerinthus' real intention was to "improve" the Christian faith.

I paid Aphileo a visit three days ago to invite him to return to our fellowship. I was not prepared for his response. We got into a philosophical argument, and

I was out of my depth. I ended up giving him all the standard answers. But they didn't seem to apply and certainly weren't accepted. I simply didn't know what to say, John. Nothing like this has ever happened before.

I don't think this is going to be an isolated case. The religious climate is changing. The early persecutions gave the issues of faith and obedience well defined edges. But now there are so many shades of gray! I know it sounds ridiculous, but it seems harder to be a Christian now than it was under Nero's persecutions.

What triggered my writing to you is a letter from Aphileo I received yesterday. I think it speaks for itself:

Dear Gaius,

After your visit I have solidified more of my thinking. I'm not sure why I'm bothering to write this letter to you, but I thought you might appreciate the irony of it all. I can't help but wince when I think of you still delivering the church party line.[6] It is so unenlightened and ignorant of current intellectual thought. You have failed to grasp the fundamental concept that only the spirit matters and all flesh is inherently bad.[7] If you had, you would not have continued to preach fairy tales of sin, a bodily resurrection, and the assurance of one's salvation.

It strikes me that the notion of sin itself is only an invention[8] to motivate those who can't appreciate an intellectual solution to life. As Cerinthus said, sin is the product of the body, and the body is irrevocably evil. Where is the responsibility for sin? It doesn't exist, Gaius; you've been duped.

During your visit you placed so much hope on a bodily resurrection[9] (which never happened) that you appeared childish. How could a perfect God ever consent to become flesh?[10] He would cease to be perfect.

You should reconsider Cerinthus' explanation. It's much more reasonable: there was the human Jesus and the divine Christ, and the two never mixed. I've even heard it speculated that the earthly Jesus was merely an illusion,[11] created to help us comprehend spiritual realities. Doesn't it follow that any salvation we can expect is of the spirit and not the body? How vulgar to suggest that God would populate heaven with a bunch of corpses![12]

I have grown weary of simplistic solutions to life: "have faith"; "just believe";[13] "trust and obey." Who's to know if we are really saved or not? Isn't assurance just another emotional crutch for those without the mental stamina to go on? I remember your saying that salvation is by faith and not by works. If that were true, why is your assurance of salvation tied so closely to keeping the commandments? Doesn't it bother you that you feel saved when you do good works but begin to doubt your salvation when you stop or violate some ethical principle?[14] The answer is simple: salvation is not tied to a physical response, not even Christ's supposed response on a cross.[15]

I wish it had occurred to me during your visit, but there are only two possible courses of action to be taken with the body. One logical response is to merely indulge one's bodily appetites.[16] Since the body cannot be reformed, why try? Besides, isn't knowledge based on knowing not only the heights but also the depths?

The other possible response is to subdue, conform or deny the body altogether. I have heard of some who through denial are now above sin, having reached spiritual perfection.[17] Some practice asceticism, subduing the body physically, and thereby are set free from its effects. It occurs to me that there is a simpler and more efficient way of dealing with the denial of the flesh—the eradication of it. Everything else is so tiring.

I must thank you for helping me to come full circle in my thinking. I've tried all I care to try and now I simply don't care—how much freer can you be? One thought does bother me: if it follows that sin and assurance are just empty words, can love[18] and hope be any different? Perhaps I'll soon find out. Yes, the simple way is the best.

Goodbye, my foolish Gaius. May you never be troubled with a real question or doubt. If there were answers, I fear you'd never find the light[19] by which to read them.

Aphileo

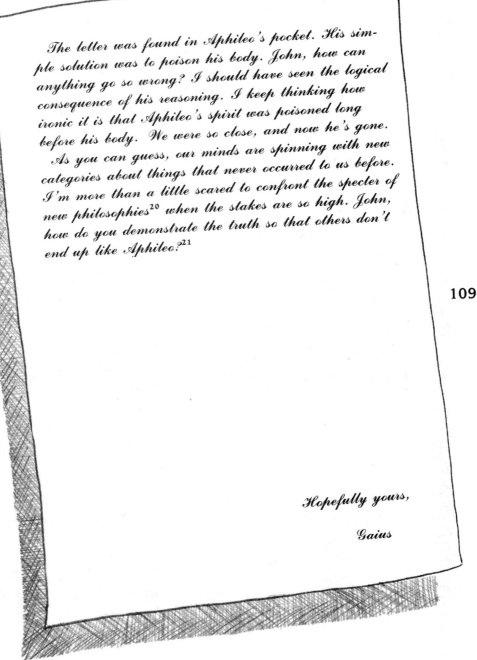

The letter was found in Aphileo's pocket. His simple solution was to poison his body. John, how can anything go so wrong? I should have seen the logical consequence of his reasoning. I keep thinking how ironic it is that Aphileo's spirit was poisoned long before his body. We were so close, and now he's gone.

As you can guess, our minds are spinning with new categories about things that never occurred to us before. I'm more than a little scared to confront the specter of new philosophies[20] when the stakes are so high. John, how do you demonstrate the truth so that others don't end up like Aphileo?[21]

109

Hopefully yours,

Gaius

NOTE TO THE READER:

It is not only the logic of an argument that makes it sound, it is the trustworthiness of the presuppositions as well. John's gospel affirmation that "the Word became flesh and dwelt among us"[22] is reiterated in his first letter along with an excellent apologetic for the assurance of salvation. He takes his readers back to the basics and builds his case on the tough realities of the Christian faith: The reality of sin[23] and the love[24] that prompted God's payment for us in the God-man Jesus.

What are the basic presuppositions of your life? Do you see them as clearly as the old Son of Thunder, or are they easily confused by the supermarket religions and philosophies of our day? The purpose of John's letter is to demonstrate that the truth is still the truth even when present alternatives have persuasive pull. As a modern-day apologist[25] put it, "Don't doubt in the darkness what you've learned in the light."

Are there any "Aphileos" in your life? John does a fine job of nailing down the basics, and that's the place to start in dealing with doubt.

110

See **Garimus' Guide for Getting in Step with the Footnotes,**

which appears on page 6.

FOOTNOTES

1. Mark 3:17.
2. Tradition holds that John was the last of the apostles and that he lived in Ephesus after the destruction of Jerusalem in A.D. 70.
3. 2 John is addressed to Gaius, who may have been a local pastor. All three of John's epistles appear closely linked, thus my speculation on the name.
4. The heresy Aphileo is involved with is called Gnosticism. The major premise of Gnosticism is that the spirit is good and that matter (or the flesh) is evil. Consequently, God, who is spirit (which is good) could not possibly have become flesh (which is bad). The implications of this reasoning reflect directly on Jesus' birth, death and resurrection. It makes the

atonement nothing more than an illusion, for Christ could not actually have died on the cross.

5. Cerinthus was a famous proponent of Gnosticism who lived during the time of John. Cerinthus insisted that Jesus was a man and Christ was a spirit. Somehow the Lord supposedly lived a Dr. Jekyll/Mr. Hyde existence. His theory makes a shambles of the atonement, for according to the theory, Jesus could die on the cross (Jesus was physical), but Christ could not, because He was spirit.

6. 1 John 5:12.

7. See note 4.

8. 1 John 1:8.

9. John 20:1—21:25 gives the fullest gospel account of the risen Lord, complete with John's own eyewitness testimony (21:24-25).

10. 1 John 1:1-2.

11. This form of Gnosticism is known as Docetism. It holds that Jesus was an illusion (a friendly ghost) who never suffered or died since He wasn't physical.

12. 1 John 3:2.

13. 1 John 5:13-15.

14. The assurance mentioned in 1 John 2:5 is experiential assurance, an inner peace and confidence of our relationship with God. John also writes of assurance based on our position in Christ (5:12). Positional assurance is the right of every believer. Experiential assurance belongs to those whose outer actions reflect an inner spiritual birth. Please note: in no way am I implying that one can lose his salvation.

15. See note 4.

16. This approach to Gnosticism simply gives up on the flesh as unsalvageable and indulges every whim. It is often called Epicureanism and accepts no responsibility for sins of the flesh.

17. Other gnostics lived very moral lives, attempting to conform an unruly flesh with the more noble spirit. And still others strove to transcend the fleshly body altogether, divorcing their spirit from the influence of the flesh and thereby attaining perfection. John's opinion is found in 1 John 1:10.

18. 1 John 4:8-21.

19. 1 John 1:5-7.

20. 1 John 2:21, 27.

21. 1 John 1:1-3.

22. John 1:14.

23. 1 John 3:8.

24. See note 18.

25. C. S. Lewis.

14
The Last Word

The following note was found on a half-baked recipe card which appears to have been an inadvertent ingredient in a very stale loaf of bread.

From the kitchen of Mother Comus

When my daughter married that big, dumb-looking fisherman, I had my doubts. I told my husband Zack that I didn't mind having a son-in-law who brought home fish—I just didn't want a son that smelled like fish. Of course, when Peter joined that group of disciples he didn't smell like fish any more. But it wasn't like he had a real job either.

I used to exercize my motherly prerogative to worry about that bunch of boys (worried myself sick one time).[1] Who'd have thought they'd ever amount to anything, much less have written all those fine letters. Ah, all's well that ends well.

Be sure to eat your vegetables,
Mother Comus

P.S. Anyone who thinks he can just read through my boys' letters without straightening his room will have me and my rolling pin to reckon with.

FOOTNOTE
1. Luke 4:38-39.

About the Author:

Gary Stanley has tried his hand as a guitar player, his knees as a janitor, his back as a carpenter and his heart as a campus director with Campus Crusade for Christ. He has survived Baylor University, Southwestern Baptist Theological Seminary and The International School of Theology (all three institutions are still intact). For the past five years, Gary has thrown his whole self into teaching New Testament Survey, numerous communication courses and directing the Institute of Biblical Studies. His next book is anybody's guess.

About the Artist:

Johnny Hawk is an unemployed falconeer who mines for gold in Alaska (when the snow melts). During the winter he thaws out in San Diego, California, with his wife and two daughters and makes ends meet by illustrating books.